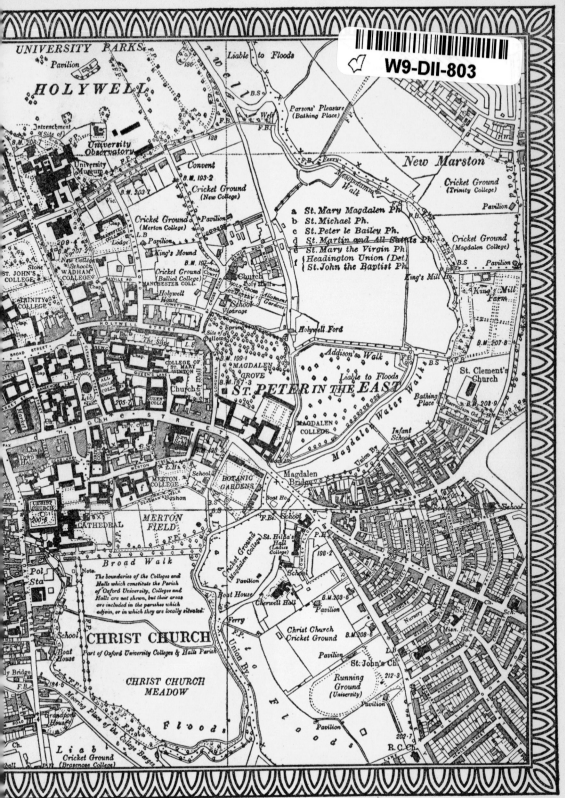

W9-DII-803

UNIVERSITY PARKS

Pavilion

HOLYWELL

Liable to Floods

B.S.

Parsons' Pleasure
(Bathing Place)

F.B. Ferry

NEW MARSTON

Cricket Ground
(Trinity College)

Pavilion

Intrenchment
& Site of

University
Observatory

University
Museum

Convent
B.M. 193·2
Cricket Ground
(New College)

Mesopotamia Walk

a St. Mary Magdalen Ph.
b St. Michael Ph.
c St. Peter le Bailey Ph.
d St. Martin and All Saints Ph.
e St. Mary the Virgin Ph.
   Headington Union (Det.)
f St. John the Baptist Ph.

Cricket Ground
(Magdalen College)

Pavilion

B.S.

Vic.

B.M. 203·7

Cricket Ground
(Merton College)

Pavilion

L.B

Pavilion

King's Mound

B.M. 197·

Cricket Ground
(Balliol College)
MANCHESTER COLL.

Holywell
House

Jowett Walk

Church
Holy Trinity

School

Vicarage

King's Mill Fm.

King's Mill
Farm

B.M. 207·8

Holywell Ford

Addison's Walk

Liable to Floods

St. Clement's
Church

ST. JOHN'S
COLLEGE

TRINITY COLLEGE

Chap.

Site of
Willows

B.M. 199·1

MAGDALEN
GROVE

Bathing
Place

B.M. 203·9

COLLEGE OF
ST. MARY

Church

ST. PETER IN THE EAST

MAGDALEN
COLLEGE

Magdalen Water Walk

Union By.

Infant
School

Town
Hall

MERTON
COLLEGE

School

BOTANIC
GARDENS

Magdalen
Bridge

Boat Ho.

School

CHRIST
CHURCH

CATHEDRAL

MERTON
FIELD

DEADMAN WALK

F.B.

School

St. Hilda's
Hall
(Ladies'
College)

198·7

School

Pol.
Sta.

Broad Walk

Note.
The boundaries of the Colleges and
Halls which constitute the Parish
of Oxford University, Colleges and
Halls are not shown, but their areas
are included in the parishes which
adjoin, or in which they are locally situated.

Cricket Ground
(Magdalen College)

Pavilion

Cherwell Hall

B.M. 203·6

Pavilion

Nursery

Man. Ho.

School

Boat
House

Boat House

Ferry

Christ Church
Cricket Ground

B.M. 208·6

L.B

St. John's Ch.

212·3

School

Bridge

F.B.

CHRIST CHURCH

Part of Oxford University Colleges & Halls Parish

CHRIST CHURCH
MEADOW

Union By.

Floods

Running
Ground
(University)

Pavilion

Grandpont
House

Mooring Place of the College Barges

B.M. 184·9

F.P.

Floods

Pavilion

Pavilion

209·7

R.C.C.

Ch.

Lias b

Cricket Ground
(Brasenose College)

P.H.

BLACKIE & SON LIMITED

To Mavis Barnett McGann
with affectionate remembrance
Anne Weston Müller

1965

Mrs. McGann.

G 551

Radcliffe Camera

OXFORD

by D. Erskine Muir

With eight plates in colour
from paintings by
Jack Merriott R.I

BLACKIE & SON LIMITED
LONDON AND GLASGOW

LIBRARY
COLBY-SAWYER COLLEGE
NEW LONDON, NH 03257

BLACKIE & SON LIMITED
16/18 William IV Street,
Charing Cross, London, W.C.2
17 Stanhope Street, Glasgow

BLACKIE & SON (INDIA) LIMITED
103/5 Fort Street, Bombay

BLACKIE & SON (CANADA) LIMITED
Toronto

Gift 12/89

DA
690
.O9B
M87

103571

1601119

Printed in Great Britain by Blackie & Son. Ltd., Glasgow

CONTENTS

PLATES

To

My Children,

who have lived in and love Oxford

INTRODUCTORY

Oxford, one of the most famous and beautiful of all cities, offers her treasures for everyone to see. Set in lovely country, with low wooded hills on either side, and two rivers girdling her, she looks from a distance perfect, a city of grey and white shining stone, set amongst green trees and golden meadows.

She will show those who come to her, famous streets and magnificent buildings, treasures of stained glass, of great libraries, of lovely gardens. She will give a glimpse of a way of life based on the love of learning, and she will testify that from century to century she preserves the tradition of love for things of the mind.

A visitor to Oxford must make a choice. Either begin with the best, or begin with the worst and go on later to the best. That is to say, if you wish to see at first sight the beauty of Oxford, you will come in by road from London, and going down through the green arch of trees which overhangs Headington Hill, you will come straight upon Magdalen bridge, with its grey stones spanning the clear waters of the little river Cherwell, with meadows on the one hand, and on the other the glorious trees of Addison's Walk, and beyond, the deer-park. The tall pale tower of Magdalen rises high into the air, and marks the beginning of the High Street, justly famed as one of the most beautiful streets in Europe. Or, if you prefer to begin in the more usual and prosaic way, you will come by train, and leaving the station—surely one of the coldest and draughtiest ever erected—you will come into Oxford through the ugly modern Queen Street with its garish crowded shop windows and its congested flow of traffic.

Yet one very interesting sight there is, for beside the Victorian façade of the Assize Courts, and near the gloomy walls of the prison, with its iron-barred windows, there rises a great mound, grass-grown and topped with trees, and beyond it you can see a tall rough rubble-and stone-built tower, rather crumbling and decayed but still formidable. These are two of the most ancient and most interesting relics of by-gone centuries. For the great mound was raised, some say by the Saxons, when Oxford was little more than a cluster of wattle and clay huts, and may have been thrown up to protect the settlement from the Danes coming up the river. In the year 1010 the Danes did in fact succeed in capturing the place, and burnt it to the ground. In any case, if not Saxon, the mound goes back at least to very early Norman days. The great tower was built by the first Norman Governor, Robert d'Oilly, sent by William I to rule the town. For nearly nine hundred years it has stood there, at this entrance to the city. One romantic story attaches to it, for from this very tower the Conqueror's granddaughter, Matilda, threatened by her enemies, fled away at night, slipping from the tower's door and escaping across the snow carrying in her arms her baby son.

Do not be disappointed if you come this way, for the ugliness is only a screen to what lies behind. Oxford, indeed, is ashamed of this approach, of the view spoilt by the gas works as your train draws in and of the badly built area and ugly streets leading from the station.

But in either case, whether you come up the High Street from Magdalen, or up Queen Street, you will arrive at Carfax, the centre of the city, and from there you can both see some little glimpse of the beauty Oxford has to show you, and begin to realize the charm which antiquity and historical associations give to her. For Oxford's beauty is many-sided. She has the beauty of her buildings and her streets, the beauty of her colleges and their gardens, each having some character-istic of its own, she has the beauty of the stained glass in colleges and churches alike, and the beauties of learning as exemplified in her famous libraries. Here are all the glories of civilization, coming down through the ages and made manifest in this city.

No one can easily define or describe the charm of Oxford. Some are at once carried away by the splendour of her streets, but some, at first sight, find her too great and busy a city. To those it can be said that her greatest beauty is withdrawn; Oxford in one sense hides her best and you must go into the Colleges, where you find peace, and old grey walls surrounding green turf, a composition which it has been said " is as near perfect as human creation can hope to get ". If you dislike the noise of the traffic which inevitably passes through the streets of what is both a great city and one set on the main highways to West and Midlands, go to some of her lovely open spaces, the meadows of Christ Church or the tree-lined walks by the river, and you will find yourself as it were back in the peace of old times, with only the sound of birds or, at dusk, the chiming of the bells which ring out from college towers. But all will find that the more they come to know of Oxford, and the better they learn to know both her magnificent buildings and her un- expected by-ways, the more they will realize that at all times and seasons this is one of the beautiful cities of the world.

Now perhaps before embarking on any exploration, it may be noted that Oxford has her own ideas as to the names by which her streets and colleges shall be popularly known, and her own pronunciation of some. Thus, three of her main streets are always called " The High ", " The Broad ", " The Cornmarket "—never " street ". The colleges you must speak of as " Trinity", not Trinity College, and " St. John's ", and " Worcester ", with one solitary exception—New College is always given that name in full, never called " New ". Similarly, the Shel- donian Theatre (which is a University place of assembly, not a place of amusement) is called " The Sheldonian ", and the Ashmolean Museum " The Ashmolean ". As to pronunciation, Magdalen is called " Mawdlin ", to true Oxonians " St. Aldate's " is " St. Olds ". And perhaps it is as well to explain here that the young men and girls, up at Oxford to study, are called " undergraduates ", since they do not graduate, that is gain their degrees, until the end of their three-year course. The senior members of the University, teachers and lecturers, are " Fellows " of their college, and are popularly known as " Dons ".

OXFORD'S STREETS AND BUILDINGS

Some people grow confused in their efforts to grasp, in a short time, the interest and loveliness of Oxford, by the very fact that these are so varied. Some leave her with a vague feeling of dissatisfaction, of worry lest they have missed something, or have muddled and tired themselves in their efforts to appreciate all. For Oxford has to be known, and it is sometimes hard to find her treasures. Those who have lived there, and do know her, often find it difficult to decide what it is that most rouses the sense of beauty and admiration, and what is the charm which she exercises over no matter how long a passage of time. Yet that charm once felt, that beauty once appreciated, the memory never dies away. Memory will re-create in the mind's eye pictures of her outward beauties; spires and towers and domes will shine out against the blue sky, or be silhouetted against the mist of autumn dusk. Countless visions will rise up and if revisited will be found to retain all their old charm. Imagination will evoke from the past the figures of many great men and women, kings and queens, scholars and poets, men of religion, men of action, soldiers and states-men, who all have moved about these ancient places. Oxford always keeps her hold on those who know her well, but it is possible too, for those who can pay her only a short visit, to find out her most pleasing characteristics, and to see, even in a brief time, things that can never be forgotten. One cannot see all Oxford in a day, but one can get an idea both of the richness of her outward charms, and a realization that here is a place where for a thousand years mankind has lived, and where at every turn there are associations with great figures of the past.

The easiest and clearest way to retain in memory what one has seen, is perhaps to take various aspects of Oxford separately, not to wander to and fro vaguely. Let us then first walk through her streets, and see in outline what they contain, then let us enter the colleges and visit their gardens.   Afterwards we can consider what special thing we wish to study—her great libraries, the glories of her stained glass, the silver and jewels of her college treasures ; or visit her quiet open spaces, her meadow and riverside walks.

Let us make a clear plan, and let us begin by going through her main streets, for walking along them one comes to realize many of her characteristics.   We can see the variety of her famous buildings, we can note the marvellous harmony of their grouping, the effect they make against the skyline.   We can get a general idea of what she has to offer us, and then we can consider in more detail what we choose.

The centre of the University city lies at Carfax, where her four main streets meet.   Indeed Carfax is derived from the Norman French Carre-four or Quatre Voies.   Once a very lovely stone conduit with carvings and pinnacles stood here.   But as far back as 1756 this was held to obstruct the traffic. So it was removed to the park at Nuneham Courtney. It is so beautiful, and so antique, that the proposers of the " modern plan " for Oxford suggest it should be brought back to Oxford and re-erected in the wide space of the Broad where a not very ornamental or impressive taxi shelter at present stands.   At Carfax, where now the vast stream of modern traffic surges noisily along, still stands part of the ancient church of St. Martin.   Most of the church has been pulled down within the last sixty years, but the rough old tower still remains, and watches, as it has done for over 700 years, the passage of man. It is one of the oldest of Oxford's many towers; its rubble-built top may be a remnant of Saxon work.   Certainly it dates back to the days of the Norman Conquest when Robert d'Oilly came as the first Norman governor in 1086 to a city which Domesday Book tells us had 500 houses left out of 1000, the rest being in ruins after some unknown disaster. He repaired the ruined houses, and either repaired or rebuilt St. Martin's tower.

Stand by that tower, with ugly Queen Street behind you, and you can see the plan of the city.   To your right is the broad street called St. Aldate's, entirely dominated here by the view of the glorious Tom Tower of Christ Church.   In front of you begins the world-renowned High Street, and to your left runs the Cornmarket which, though without any college buildings, and looking like nothing but the shopping street it is, will lead you in a few moments to Oxford's other glorious street, St. Giles.

Before setting out to go through the streets, pause and look up and notice the effect of the towers and spires which rise above the roof tops. You can see the whole of Tom Tower, and behind it the towers and spires of Christ Church Hall, and of the Cathedral, with beyond this again the vast bulk of Merton Tower. You can see the great dome of the Radcliffe, the tall spire of St. Mary's and the pinnacles of All Souls. Indeed few realize that the roof-top level of Oxford is extraordinarily beautiful and varied, and it is worth while to try and envisage it. These spires, domes, turrets, roofs of colleges and ancient houses, silhouetted against the sky, give you a clue to one of Oxford's great charms, her " infinite variety ", and this holds good as well of the buildings and streets below.

Take, as an example, the great High Street. The solid piles of the colleges, with their massive arched gateways, are jostled and interspersed with eighteenth-century houses, now shops, with plain elegant fronts and tall sash windows. The tall classical spire of the City Church, All Saints, stands next to, and contrasts with, the magnificent mass of the fourteenth-century spire of the University Church, St. Mary-the-Virgin. The ornate Renaissance porch of St. Mary's, with its " barley-sugar " twisted columns, looks across to the high gables of fifteenth-century houses. Yet all blend together in harmony. The shops themselves in their turn show how ancient and modern combine in one whole. There can scarcely be found one modern building in the whole street, yet the old shops, with their upper storeys and their gable ends, much as they have been for many hundred years, show in their windows the blending of modern tastes with ancient tradition. For one may display the robes and hoods worn by members of the university, varying in type and colour, but all derived from robes worn in the Middle Ages. Another may house one of those fascinating book shops in which Oxford abounds. Here rare old volumes may be arranged alongside modern works, a page of an illuminated manuscript or sheet of ancient music may be alongside nineteenth-century colour prints of horses or birds, or flowers. Here, outside the shop, are ranged those eternally tempting shelves of second-hand books. If you wish to catch one particular flavour of Oxford life, go inside and browse around, as you will find many others doing. You can look, read, and in the end walk out after as long a study of the enthralling volumes as you choose. No one will disturb you as you prowl around. Indeed many will tell you how they have spent happy hours reading through these books—the proprietor does not check this practice. Many an Oxonian will recall those wet afternoons, when outdoor occupations fail, when he wandered from shelf to shelf, taking down and dipping into any-thing he fancied, searching for treasures unlikely as it is he will find any, and years after will think of the time so spent as one of the happiest of his memories of Oxford. Or again, as this is predominantly a " man's " city, the windows of the shops will not be such as to attract lingering crowds of women shoppers. They will display the gaiety of goods showing the efforts of the young man of to-day to brighten his appearance with multi-coloured scarves, handkerchiefs, socks, dressing-gowns. Even the old tobacconist's, with its overhanging front, shows goods gaily emblazoned with college crests. And, by way of further diversity, conspicuous stands that famous old inn, the Mitre, with its picturesque shallow bow-windows, its small panes of glass, its gay geraniums over the old doorway, looking perfectly at home and in keeping with the church it adjoins and the colleges around.

Pilgrims to Oxford usually turn their steps first towards the great college of Christ Church, and often when they sort out their memories of the city, it is Christ Church they most vividly recall. From Carfax, St. Aldate's broad street slopes gently downhill with an almost imper-ceptible curve, and there, so placed that the wonderful tower of the great gateway dominates the whole view, stands this symbol of many-sided life, college and cathedral, both illustrating the passing of cen-turies and the gifts each generation brings to them. Christ Church looms up near at hand as you stand at Carfax, and as you go towards it, perhaps you may notice, and not altogether with favour, the ornate stone carvings of the City Hall. Yet taste is often varying, and intent on the accepted beauties of older buildings, we may not be adequate judges of the new. Many foreigners have been known to hail this City Hall as beautiful, and to some it seems almost familiar, for it resembles old Dutch and Flemish town halls. Indeed one should perhaps approach Oxford architecture with humility since we now bitterly condemn the Victorians for destroying, in the certainty of their own taste, things we should think beautiful. What pleases one generation is disliked by another, or may later return to favour.

There has never been any change, however, in the admiration felt for Christ Church, the largest and one of the most beautiful of the colleges. Its great scale gives it splendour, for in almost every respect it is overwhelming. Its quadrangle is the largest, its dining-hall the largest, its " chapel " even is the largest in Oxford, for it is in truth the ancient Cathedral. Size is of course no measure of beauty, but Christ Church has such glorious proportions, is so magnificent in its grandeur that its impression is overwhelming.

" Tom Tower " as the great gate tower is called is reckoned incomparable. It was created by the genius of two very different men, Cardinal Wolsey and, a century and a half later, Sir Christopher Wren. Wolsey built the turrets which stand on either side of the gate, whose high wooden doors, unlike those of any other college, are kept open, since the cathedral which lies in the corner of the quadrangle must be available at all times. Wolsey's fall left his building incomplete, and when Wren became architect, he brought ideas very different from those of the Tudor time. He designed small graceful cupolas for the tops of Wolsey's turrets, he built the beautiful eight-sided tower, and rising from that, one of the loveliest and most delicate of domes. The louvres on those eight sides show us that this is essentially a bell-chamber, though many, at a casual glance, take it to be merely an unusually slender and lovely form of tower. For Wren was building for a great occupant, " Big Tom " the famous bell, a couple of centuries older than the tower, brought from Osney Abbey when Henry VIII dissolved the monasteries. Just as Wren's tower often remains in the mind as an outstanding feature of Oxford's architecture, so the sound of that great bell lingers in the memory and brings with it endless associations.

Every night, at five minutes past nine, the deep tones toll out 101 strokes, one for each of the 101 scholars of the college. This has a special significance and not only to the men of Christ Church, for as the last note dies away, every college in Oxford closes its gates, and late-comers must ring for the porters to open. The boom rings out over the whole city, and dwellers in the northern part of Oxford say that when they hear those deep tones borne very clearly on the breeze they know rain is on the way.

Beyond the tower you can see glimpses of green trees from Christ Church Broad Walk, or a gleam from the brilliant flowers of the war memorial gardens. Till 1929 dilapidated old houses stood there, but Christ Church cleared what was almost a slum area and made the lovely garden, open to all, as part of its memorial to the men of the college who fell in the 1914 war. You can guess a little what the shabby old houses were like, for opposite there still stands a decayed old fifteenth-century house. You can see too what can be rescued and given fresh life, for there is the old Tudor house of Bishop King, once almost a ruin, now a place of beauty. And you should look at a queer little corner shop, still surviving opposite Christ Church garden, for that little shop is said to be the original which gave Lewis Carroll the idea of the immortal shop in *Through-the-Looking-Glass* where the old lady, so like a sheep, tantalized Alice in her efforts to buy an egg. Lewis Carroll (Professor Dodgson was his real name) was a mathematical don at Christ Church—his attractive portrait hangs in the great hall—and many a time as he passed out beneath Tom Tower he must have glanced across at the humble little shop over the way. This is a perfect example of the contrast in association which strikes you so often in Oxford, the splendour of Wolsey's great college, the glory of Wren's tower, and the humble little shop—the two brought together by the genius of one man, who though learned of the learned, won fame as the writer of the most famous amongst all children's fairy tales.

Pass on beyond the great college, and as you do so, look back and see the glorious view which the memorial garden has opened up, the college wall, the great dining-hall and the tower of the cathedral. Then you will come to " Folly Bridge ", a very important bridge of Oxford, and one which at any time provides a study in contrasts. Folly Bridge crosses the Isis, as this reach of the Thames is called. On the right-hand side you lean over and see a black, dirty, sluggish stream, surrounded by gasworks and breweries, and fouled by industry. Yet on some days it has a strange touch of beauty too, for the dark oily surface, surprisingly enough, is beloved by the swans, who sail up from the clearer reaches of the Thames to collect here, twenty, thirty, and more at a time, and their white glistening plumage shines out against the dark water. Folly Bridge is said to be the place of the original " ford of the ox ", which gives the city its name, and as such has special interest.

If you turn to the other side of the bridge you find there a very different scene. This is the reach of the river on which the boats of the colleges row their races. The water here runs clear and bright, up to Iffley Lock, past trees and meadows, in summer golden with butter-cups, and it is here that Oxford stages one of its gayest festivals. All the year round the college " barges " lie moored along the banks of Christ Church meadows, overshadowed by tall trees. Here in misty autumn the crews practise, and if you walk then along the tow-path to lovely Iffley, with its famous little Norman church, overlooking lock and river, the air is full of the injunctions to the crews and the cry of " in-out, in-out " issued by the cox. But when the close of May comes along this springs to glorious life. The barges—resplendent in gilt and paint, with their carved figure-heads or shields blazoned with college arms, and each flying its college flag—are filled with gay crowds. " Eights " week is the occasion for the races between the various col-leges, and on the last day, the coxes of those boats in the final division (that is to say the best) have, tucked into the front of their blazers, bouquets of flowers representing their college colours. So you will see them go by, with Magdalen cox wearing a great bunch of white lilies, New College purple and yellow iris, Pembroke cornflowers, red, white and blue, and so on. In bright sunshine, the colours, the shouting, the gay excitement, make it most charming and thrilling, like a carnival.

Thus St. Aldate's gives you a picture in miniature of what you will find everywhere in this city, splendour, the charm of ancient buildings, gardens, and the gaiety and zest of youth.

Now, from St. Martin's, Carfax, you look straight across to the High Street, and if you set out to walk along it, you can see how arresting indeed it is. Not only, as you go along, are your eyes caught by the varied beauty and richness of the buildings on either side, but you realize that the whole plan and structure of the street is unique. Its great beauty is due partly to its proportions, the width of the roadway

The High

G 551

fitting exactly with the height of colleges, gateways, gables and towers, partly to the curve which moves on in a line always drawing the eye from one beauty to another. The High Street is most beautiful perhaps at dusk, when traffic slackens, and when every building rises into a darkening sky. But it is beautiful too when the sun lightens the grey stone, or early on a Sunday morning, when a shower has cleared the street and for a brief moment as the clouds pass by you may glimpse solitude and emptiness and see what this was before modern traffic obscured its glorious lines.

Here, along one side, you wander past University College, where Shelley had his brief taste of University life, before his college found it necessary to expel him for his " atheistic " pamphlet. You can see a copy of that pamphlet in the cases of the Bodleian Library, and be reminded—as you look on it, and at that more precious relic, the book found on his body after his death by drowning in the far-off Mediterranean—of how Shelley too loved Oxford, and wandered up Shotover Hill, or talked (as all young men in Oxford do) of an evening, sitting in his room overlooking the quadrangle, warmed by his roaring fire and by the companionship of his friends. University College claims to be the first college to be " organized as a corporate body ", though its buildings are not the oldest, for the founder of Merton was quicker to lay his foundations and to erect his walls. But it has a special charm for many (especially Americans) since they say it was founded by Alfred the Great—though stern fact says it was founded in 1249—when William of Durham left " 300 marks " to the university to build a Hall. Be that as it may, University College stands on perhaps the best spot to show the glories of this famous street.

Across the way there is a whole line of beautiful buildings. Next to the University Church, St. Mary's, with its ornate Renaissance porch, its fourteenth-century tower and spire rising massively above, is the typical collegiate building of All Souls, a college which as we shall see later is quite different from all others in its membership. Its architecture, however, is just what you might expect in a college. There is the arch of the entrance, with big wooden doors, kept closed save for very great occasions, and with the little wicket door through which you step to find the porter's lodge. There are the mullioned windows, with the stone " hoods " running above them; there are the gables and dormer windows. And looking through the open door you can see the square court (called a quadrangle, and shortened down to quad) round which are built the rooms of members of the college, and you can notice the wonderful green turf which usually fills the centre of Oxford's quads and which is a source of pride and glory.

Beyond All Souls, another college strikes a different note. Queen's College is in the " classical " style favoured by the eighteenth century. It fits most wonderfully into the curve which the great street makes here, and over the gateway the open cupola, which protects a statue of Queen Caroline, the brilliant wife of George II, breaks the skyline most charmingly. Then, almost lost amongst the stately pile of church and college, but giving a very homely and warming touch, there stands neighbouring Queen's a group of little gable-fronted houses, still retaining their many-paned windows, and these in turn give way to the culminating glory of Magdalen and its tower, rising 150 feet into the air, guarding the bridge over the river. You will not be satisfied if you walk only once down the High, and if you come back from Magdalen you will find yourself a prey to an indecision which seizes everyone. From which direction, and from which side, is the beauty of the street most striking? No one ever answers that question definitely.

Leave now the broad High Street itself, and go into the by-ways which branch off from it, and you find yourself in a different world, for in these little lanes you lose the noise of traffic, the spectacle of modern life, and you can step right back into the Middle Ages. Such, for example, is Magpie Lane, where you will find almost a tiny village of old dwelling-houses and gardens, or take your way down Oriel Lane, where the gabled houses with their overhanging fronts seem almost to touch the walls opposite. Turn and look back, and you may see, framed by the deep shadows of the lane, the front of St. Mary's brilliantly lit by the sunshine, a quite unforgettable glimpse. This lane leads to a small triangular open space, one of Oxford's most charming quarters. Here is a small row of old houses, plaster-fronted, with gay little gardens. To one side is Oriel itself, looking across to the back of Christ Church. This part of Christ Church is in the classical style, and is called " Peckwater " from the name of an old inn which once stood there. Towering up is the great " Canterbury Gate ", leading into Peck-water Quad—completely Roman in its massive outline. It is always difficult to see *how* these utterly various styles harmonize—gabled cottages, medieval college walls, classical archways—yet harmonize they do, perhaps because they show the continuity of Oxford with each century represented, because it is a natural growth and therefore satisfactory.

Follow the sharp twist of the road round the corner opposite Can-terbury Gate and you are in Merton Street, a little road running past Corpus Christi College and Merton, and twisting round at the far end to emerge into the High Street, near Magdalen. It is beautiful and still, and usually empty of all traffic, though only a stone's-throw away roars the noise of the High. This little street retains its medieval character. It still keeps its old cobblestones, and at the far end a few old gabled houses lean outwards, facing the green trees of the Fellows' garden, which overhang the wall. Merton is the oldest of all the colleges, as far as its buildings go. It was begun in 1274, and as that was before Wykeham had fully evolved the idea of large quadrangles, Merton is a haphazard arrangement of small courts, narrow passages, old arch-ways. Here in the little street you breathe the very air of antiquity. High above rises the vast bulk of the great square tower of the chapel, always a dominating feature of the city when seen from afar. Merton Chapel was originally meant to be a great church, and was indeed used as the parish church of old St. John's, but only chancel and tower were completed. It was therefore planned on a far bigger scale than any college chapel, and the bells which sound from the tower ring out more deeply and strongly than those of any other (since " Big Tom " does not " chime ", he " tolls "). At evening especially the little street, with its deep shadows, its emptiness and silence, is one of Oxford's treasures, and evokes as can no other the spirit of the past. At dark too, standing in Merton Street and looking towards Christ Church, you will see the Canterbury Gate looming like a great Roman triumphal arch, and the contrast between that massive splendour and the small medieval lane is indeed dramatic.

Let us turn now from these quiet narrow ways, to what is the true centre of the University, as Carfax is of the city. Behind St. Mary-the-

Virgin's lies the Radcliffe Square. It is a large square quite without
traffic, part of it still cobbled, and its sides enclosed by four great
buildings—the austere north front of St. Mary's; All Souls, with a tall
wrought-iron gate through which you can gaze at the green quadrangle,
with Hawksmoore's fantastic crocketed spires rising above the splendid
lines of Codrington's Library; Brasenose, with the actual " brazen
nose " which gives the college its name, fixed to the wooden doors that
here, as in every college, close the gateway; and the long lines of the
Bodleian Library. In the centre rises the Radcliffe Camera, with its
huge dome. This is a building endowed by one of Oxford's great
benefactors, the same Radcliffe who founded the hospital which bears
his name. The Camera is now the " reading-room " for the Bodleian
Library, and true students, in these days of a packed, overcrowded
university, scramble for places where they may sit and study the books
from the Bodleian itself, since the statutes of the library lay down that
no book may be taken out of the building, and all must be studied
within its walls.

The Bodleian Library—these are words to conjure with. This is in
truth one of the world's great libraries. It is vast in the number of its
books, for besides the great collections bequeathed or acquired in the
past, it is one of the libraries to which every British publisher must
send a copy of every book and every periodical he publishes. To hold
these immense numbers great underground places have been built,
and thousands upon thousands of volumes lie in the vaults below the
neighbouring streets. To this great store of learning come scholars
from every part of the world, and its treasures are indeed beyond
price. Perhaps the word " library " may seem dull to those who are not
" literary-minded " or fond of books, but the Bodleian is housed in a
most beautiful building, and has moreover great historical associations.
Go across the quaint cobblestones of the square, and opposite St.
Mary's you see a modest-looking archway. Go through and you are
in what is called the " Schools Square ", since in old times the " schools "
into which the University was divided—Arts, Divinity, and so on—
were here. You can still see their titles emblazoned over the small
doorways. You stand here in a courtyard with grey walls stretching
up to the sky. You are enclosed in a little world where silence reigns.

G 551

Tom Tower, Christ Church

The tall grey walls have few windows, and they are " panelled " as it were with mouldings in stone. The great Schools Tower reproduces in its pillars and capitals the " five orders " of architecture, and in a niche high up on the tower stands the figure of King James I, holding in each of his hands a book, which he presents to two kneeling figures, Religion and Fame. This was meant to be a compliment to a king who, himself a learned man, earned fame by his patronage of the Authorized Version of the Bible. Here, roofed in by the sky, surrounded by a building dedicated to learning, you feel you have stepped back through the centuries. Sir Thomas Bodley founded the library in the days of Queen Elizabeth (in 1508), and you will see his bust if you go out through the great arch of the Clarendon Buildings to the " New Bodleian ". Or you may visit Merton Chapel, where he was buried, and see his contemporary monument. And in the " picture gallery " of the library, now a little museum of special treasures, there is the great iron chest in which, in Bodley's day, the money for the library was kept.

Bodley, though he gave his wealth and his name to the library, incorporated a far older collection, that of " Duke Humphrey ". Humphrey of Gloucester was the youngest son of King Henry IV. He loved books, and they were his chief interest, unlike his more celebrated warlike brother, King Henry V, and when he died he left all his manuscripts to Oxford. They were housed in a room, built in 1480, called then, and still called, " Duke Humphrey's Library ". With its beautiful wooden " bays ", its arcaded galleries, and above all its painted ceiling, this is one of the most beautiful rooms imaginable. To find it is not perhaps the easiest thing in the world. You must make your way across the " Schools Square " and, if you have come from the archway of the Radcliffe, on your left, in the corner, you will see a small quite inconspicuous door. Go in, and undeterred by apparent improbability (for this is actually the only way to the library) go up several flights of a steep narrow stair. You will then find yourself faced by an incongruous glass door. Push this open, and you are in "Bodley", faced with all the richness and glory of "Duke Humphrey", for so the first half of the incomparable room is called. Here in cases are spread out some of the most beautiful, and rarest, of the manuscripts, medieval, Persian, Arabic, Indian, specimens of civilizations going back a thousand years. You may see too a few specially English treasures—verses in Milton's own writing, the exercise books which Edward VI and his sister Elizabeth wrote when they were children, and one case of touching interest to those who love the poet Shelley. In this, bequeathed specially in recognition of the fact that Shelley was an Oxonian, are the relics of his drowning (the watch he was wearing and the book found in his pocket), and the guitar which Jane Williams played and of which he wrote in one of his last poems " To a Lady Playing a Guitar ". If you have time, spend a moment or two and look at the little " gallery " half-way up the staircase, which includes amongst many other treasures a chair made from the wood of the ship *Golden Hind* in which Drake sailed round the world; here too is a rare treasure, one of the authentic copies of the death mask of the great Napoleon. Yes, Bodley can please all tastes, and its beauty is undying.

The other side of the Bodleian brings you to the " Broad "—a short, very wide street whose outstanding feature is the Sheldonian Theatre. Possibly here Oxford gives a touch of light relief, after the studious severity of the great library. For the Sheldonian, whose architect was Christopher Wren, is the building where university ceremonies—such as the granting of degrees—are held, and some unknown architect surrounded the approach by a series of gigantic heads, mounted on tall pillars, representing in theory the great philosophers Plato, Aristotle, and so on. In past days unruly undergraduates would amuse themselves by climbing up and decorating these venerable heads with highly unsuitable headgear. Again, we can derive amusement from some of the details of the ceremonies which take place there. For when M.A.s (Masters of Arts) go to receive their degrees, they kneel before the Vice-Chancellor, who touches their heads with the Bible—and this you can see duly represented in the carvings on the big modern buildings of the Examination Schools in the High Street.

Structurally the Sheldonian (it takes its name from the founder, Dr. Sheldon) is most interesting. It was built by Wren to illustrate one of his theories, the " geometrical Flat ", and being semicircular gives it an odd appearance to most eyes. Strange, too, is its ceiling, which is in a freakish way painted to give the illusion of a painted canvas supported by ropes like an awning. Its chief interest really lies in the ceremonies which take place within it, for it is here that all the great university official meetings take place. Wren himself was proud of his ingenuity, and took his friend John Evelyn to see how well he had succeeded in his curious design.

The remaining one of Oxford's large streets is St. Giles. It is in appearance not a true " street ". It is a broad avenue, with a wide " centre-way " bordered with very large trees, and with further wide stretches on either hand. Thus it has the appearance of a great open space. Down the centre-way rolls the traffic streaming out to Banbury, of Banbury Cross fame, to Woodstock and the palace of Blenheim, on beyond to Stratford-on-Avon and the west. The spreading green of the trees, the group of elms of what is called the " terrace " before St. John's, counteract the impression of a great traffic road. The spire of the Martyr's Memorial stands hard by Balliol, and looks down St. Giles to face the tall cross of the war memorial, and where the two streams of traffic divide to the west and the midlands, the vista is closed by the ancient little church of St. Giles. The fifteenth- and eighteenth-century houses stand far back even from the avenue of trees; the only shops are a cluster of gabled houses with crooked fronts. Old prints show St. Giles as a country way, with flocks of sheep being driven along, and the space and the greenery gives even to-day an air more of domestic life than anything else.

Here in the first week of September comes a strange transformation. For by immemorial custom, at that time is held " St. Giles's Fair ". The whole great road is closed to traffic for three days, and brilliant colours of " merry-go-rounds ", of swings and towers, fill the great space. Children and parents come in from all the country round, and the often quoted " city of dreaming spires " becomes in this place, for once in the year, a city of fun and noise and colour.

There are more sombre tones to set against the gaiety of the Fair. For St. Giles recalls and commemorates some of the saddest pages in English history. Mary Tudor, when she resolved to stamp out Protestantism, had specially singled out three famous men, Archbishop Cranmer and Bishops Latimer and Ridley. Latimer and Ridley were brought in procession to the spot where the stake had been set up, outside Balliol. Ridley wore his bishop's robes, Latimer, now a very old man, wore a grey gown and girdle. Latimer, as they were tied to the stake, uttered the famous words, " Be of good cheer, for we shall this day light a candle which shall not soon be put out." On the spot where they suffered now rises the " Martyr's Memorial ". Cranmer, from his prison in the Bocardo close by, saw them pass, and some say he was forced to watch their agonizing sufferings from the tower of St. Mary Magdalen's hard by. He himself, after being tried in the Divinity School and making his abjuration of his errors in St. Mary-the-Virgin's Church, was despite that condemned to death. And in the Broad Street, then the common ditch surrounding the city wall, he too was burnt, holding his right hand first in the flames to testify that as his right hand had signed his abjuration, so he now tried to show that he detested his own cowardice. You may find, in the roadway in Broad Street nearby, opposite the main gateway of Balliol, the small brass cross which marks the site of his burning.

Again, St. John's College recalls Archbishop Laud—executed by the Long Parliament for his unpopular rule as Minister of Charles I. Laud loved St. John's and left his money to build the beautiful Canterbury Quad. His head and body after execution, in London on Tower Hill, were brought to Oxford and buried in his College Chapel. One used to be able to see the little skull cap he wore at his beheading, but " visitors " made a habit of snipping pieces out of it as " souvenirs "—so this sight is denied us.

Yet though Oxford owes its fame to the university, it still is, as it has always been, a country town, the centre of a prosperous countryside.

If you are fresh from London, or any big city, you will be fascinated by the occasional passage of a cart laden with bales of hay, the sight of a corn chandler's shop, or an old-fashioned saddler's. You will notice the country-people who come in to shop on market days and you can find a corner of Oxford which is a centre of rural life still. Behind Queen Street and the Castle lies the " open market ". Here you find cows, pigs, poultry, all being bargained for, just as in any country place. You will find stalls with crockery, clothes, dress material, with loud-voiced men offering bargains. And you will find, round the market area, little old streets full of picturesqueness. You may be startled to look up and see on the corner that the name of one street is " High Street "—but you are here in the old quarter of St. Thomas, which has firmly stuck to its own High Street, placidly ignoring its great neighbour. You can see there a most wonderful large early Jacobean house in red brick, with stone pediments and graceful urns. To reach this district you pass over " Quaking Bridge ", where a little river runs, with water-plants growing in it. And you can go on along the little streets and come to " Hythe Bridge ", which has a stone-paved terrace between the river and a row of little old cottages. It is a fascinating area, though little known to visitors.

If you wish to see another distinctive little corner, find out " Hell's Passage ", whose official name is St. Helen's Passage. It begins as an incredibly narrow alley, just below the " Bridge of Sighs ", which crosses the opening of New College Lane. The tiny dark passage does not look as if it led anywhere. But follow its twists and abrupt turns, and suddenly you will come out in a small open place. Here, as if it were still in a village, stands a cosy little tavern, with old-fashioned red blinds. Beyond are tiny cottages and gardens. Only the narrowest of footpaths leads from this little corner, nestling against the old city wall and showing what a tangle of byways once was here. Go on, and the alley suddenly turns abruptly under an arch, and you find yourself out in the picturesque " Bath Place ", in whose little gabled houses Rossetti and William Morris and Burne Jones once lived.

COLLEGES AND UNIVERSITY LIFE

Now, having obtained an outline of the old city, let us turn to that " hidden " or withdrawn aspect, let us go out of the streets and go to the colleges. Oxford began (in 1167) as a place where poor scholars could come to hear great teachers. The scholars lived either in lodgings or gathered in small " halls ". Then came the first benefactors, great churchmen mostly, who began to build or endow " colleges " where students should live—Wykeham, Bishop of Winchester, and Archbishop Chichele, and Bishop Waynflete and the others. Two colleges owe their rise to women, Balliol and Wadham, for when John Balliol died, his widow Devorguilla carried out his wishes and was the true benefactor of his college, while Wadham was founded by Dorothy Wadham. In courts and halls and chapels is found the essence of the life of the university.

The colleges of Oxford, and of Cambridge, have in the course of centuries developed their own way of life distinct in many respects from that of other universities. Here, unlike many of the modern and of the foreign universities, the students live in the colleges. Before the 1914 war, an undergraduate would have a " set ", that is to say a bedroom and a sitting-room. The " Scout ", as Oxford calls the men who carry out the domestic work of a college, would carry up hot water for a saucer-bath to the bedroom, and would bring up breakfast and lunch to the rooms. Nowadays that is all altered. The number of students is far larger, and a very great proportion now have State Scholarships, and in general the modern undergraduate has not much money to spare. So life is far simpler than it was forty years ago. " Sets " of rooms are shared, and all take their meals together in the college dining-hall. Most college halls have the same characteristics, too. Long tables stretch the length of the room with benches for the undergraduates. These are of wood, and rumour says that when, after the 1939 war, Russian delegates attended a conference in Oxford and used the college halls, they were extremely contemptuous of the discomfort of the hard backless benches, ignoring the antiquity of the practice and the fact that many of the benches are themselves centuries old. The "High Table", raised on a dais, runs across the top of the hall, and here the Fellows of the colleges dine—but they are provided with comfortable padded chairs. Each college hangs portraits of its founders, and these are added to throughout the centuries. Kings and Queens, soldiers and statesmen, scholars and clergy, all are represented. Some of the most famous are in Christ Church great hall, where the Holbein portrait of Henry VIII swaggers over the High Table. Two specially interesting portraits are to be seen in Jesus College. This was founded in 1571 by a Welshman (Hugh ap Rice), on a site given by Queen Elizabeth, herself of Welsh descent. Her portrait is one of the best of her existing, though it had remained unknown as such until a recent commission discovered its merits. She hangs in her jewelled pomp on the wall, and nearby is one of the most famous of the college's sons in modern times—Lawrence of Arabia. A strange pair to keep company on those walls, but perhaps they share a good deal in common in their courage, enterprise and ability.

New College is one of the colleges which always pleases those who visit Oxford, for its lovely gardens are bordered by the remnants of the old city wall. Indeed, when the founder, William of Wykeham, planned his foundation in 1379, he was only allowed to build on the site on condition that he kept the city wall in repair. A tale goes round that during the 1939 war, a joker (certainly a former member of New College) called the attention of the War Office to the fact that the repair of the wall was "inadequate for defence", and the college was notified it must "put things in repair"—or forfeit their lease.

Another story, true this time, gives an extraordinary example of the immense length of time which can be spanned by incidents in the life of a college. Wykeham was originally an architect and surveyor of the royal castles. He took holy orders and became Bishop of Winchester, and he planned to endow a college at Oxford, dedicated (as was his famous school at Winchester) to St. Mary the Virgin. Over New College gateway you may see a most beautiful group with the

exquisite figure of the Virgin in the centre and with the founder and
an angel on either side. Now Wykeham is famous as the true designer
of what came to be the accepted model for college buildings. He himself designed the "front" quadrangle, placing the rooms for the
Warden over the entrance arch with the idea that the Warden could
keep an eye on the comings and goings of his students, and he laid
out the college chapel and the dining-hall in one block, adjoining each
other. This meant that the east-end wall of the chapel was the "west
end" of the hall, so there is no "east window". Instead there is the
splendid reredos filled with sculptured figures. Wykeham's chapel and
hall were both originally built with a flattish low-pitched roof suited to
the style of the buildings. The chapel roof was found to be decayed and was removed in the early nineteenth century by Wyatt, and
later Sir Gilbert Scott replaced Wyatt's plaster-work with what is now
recognized as a totally unsuitable high-pitched roof. The hall roof,
however, lasted longer, and was left untouched by the Victorian Scott.
When, some twenty years ago, it was found that the beams were really
decayed, the Fellows, anxious to avoid Scott's mistake, sought advice
everywhere as to how they could obtain beams big enough to take a
low-pitched roof. No one seemed able to provide them, and then in
a moment of inspiration, the Fellows called the "head forester" to a
meeting. New College owns lands and woods, and when the forester
appeared, he was told why his opinion was being asked. He was a
little old man with white hair and sparkling blue eyes. Those eyes lit
up with joy and he exclaimed, "Thank God I've lived to see this day!"
Called on to explain, he told how from father to son the tradition had
been handed down that when the old beams gave out "The Founder's
Wood" would be ready. And so it proved. Wykeham, all those centuries ago, had calculated the probable life of his beams, the time it
would take for the timber to grow to maturity, and "Founder's Wood"
was planted by him and duly provided the timbers for the replacement.

Of the "great" colleges, which all people who come to Oxford wish
to see, New College vies with Magdalen and Christ Church—and in
each case the variety of Oxford's charms is clear. At New College
you wander instinctively through the "front" quad to the "Garden
Quad", which in summer blazes with the colour of its flowers behind

G 551

Peckwater Library

the beautiful iron grilles. The chapel has its very large " ante-chapel ",
where in Wykeham's day the scholars could write and study in the
light of the great west window. Let us leave for a later chapter the
beauties of the glass, but it is worth while to look for a moment
at the war memorials of the 1914 war, for there is a special note sounded
here. All along the south wall of the ante-chapel are those heart-rend-
ing long lists of the young men of the college who lost their lives in that
war. Next to these lists is a plaque to commemorate the German Rhodes
scholars who had been at New College. For the original terms of Cecil
Rhodes' bequest laid down that a certain number of German young
men should, along with young men from the Dominions, come to
Oxford. These particular Germans, after their three years at Oxford,
had gone back to Germany just as the 1914 war broke out, and found
themselves fighting as enemies the country where they had studied.
The plaque gives their names and recalls that " These also died for
their country ". The words, and the two sets of names put side by
side, seem to ring out the true spirit of Christianity and to emphasize
the brotherhood of man which, pushing aside differences and over-
coming death itself, remains eternal.

New College has the most beautiful cloisters in Oxford, built apart
from the rest of the college, near the chapel, and rising above that is
the old Founder's Tower, built to fit in with the city wall. Unbroken
peace reigns here, save for the occasional sound of the bells.

Turn away from the old entrance gate of New College, and pass
under the arch which connects the Warden's lodgings with the great
barn. That barn, built in Wykeham's day, has never needed restoration,
and the roof inside still has the old reeds and plaster. Then you will
find yourself going down one of the most peaceful and beautiful little
places. The " Lane ", as it is called, winds between the old walls first
of New College, then of Queen's, where wall-flowers grow in the cran-
nies. Pass the little ancient Church of St. Peter's-in-the-East, with a
wonderful Saxon crypt, pass the tiny St. Edmund's Hall, named after
Oxford's first saint, Edmund Rich, scholar and teacher, and from the
stillness and solitude of the lane you emerge to the roar of the High
Street traffic, swirling down over Magdalen Bridge and on to London.

Here is Magdalen, founded by Bishop Waynflete in 1458. For all its grandeur and wealth, Magdalen has no impressive entrance, but just a small arch. Go on through the cloisters with their strange fabulous monsters on the top of the buttresses. Then, in just the same way in which you might have overlooked the insignificant entrance to the college itself, you will find two or three narrow little passages opening off the north side of the cloisters. Go through these and you find yourself emerging into a glorious open space. Across the smooth green grass rise the beautiful eighteenth-century " New Buildings ". Behind and around them is the famous deer-park, where the deer lie under the shade of the great trees and where in winter they will come right up to the windows to be fed by those who are lucky enough to have rooms overlooking this paradise. Here the Cherwell divides and flows past the college. " Addison's Walk ", named after the writer, will lead you to a water-mill, and in spring the banks of the walk are brilliant with daffodils and you will see the " snake flower " or spotted fritillary, which grows wild in the water-meadows round Oxford. If you are in Oxford on May morning (1st of May) you can get up early and go down to hear the choristers of Magdalen, who have been assembled on the very top of the choir, sing a beautiful Latin hymn as the sun rises. Crowds gather nowadays, but even crowds hush their noise when the sounds begin to float sweetly down. Magdalen seems to be full of pale shining colour—the stone, the grass, the trees, the water of river and stream.

The third of the great colleges, Christ Church, is perhaps the most magnificent. Henry VIII meant to obliterate Wolsey's memory, as he confiscated his wealth, but Wolsey seems to have triumphed after all. The college was begun in 1525, and was to be called " Cardinal College ". Wolsey planned it on a vast scale. He took advantage of his own short-lived zeal for reform, and swept away amongst other small monasteries that of St. Frideswide's Priory, which had less than seven members. He destroyed most of the buildings, though he left the ancient Norman church, now the Cathedral. In its place he meant to create the greatest of colleges, and he succeeded in beginning the huge front quadrangle, where the projecting foundations, which lend so much character, show how originally a stupendous cloister was to surround the whole space. He began the hall, the largest in Oxford, and then came his fall from

power, his disgrace and death. Henry VIII, sweeping away all monasteries, allowed the last Abbot of Osney Priory to become the first bishop
of a new diocese, Oxford. He renamed Cardinal College, first Henry
VIII's College but later " The House of Christ ", hence the college is
by Oxonians called " The House ".

Later, the great bell of Osney Abbey was hung in the entrance
gateway, the bell called " Big Tom ", and thus the tower begun by
Wolsey which houses it, is called " Tom Tower " and the great quadrangle is " Tom Quad ". Christ Church differs from other colleges, in
that its college chapel is really the Cathedral, which stands half hidden
by the walls of the college. The Dean of the Cathedral is the head of
the college, and most of Tom Quad is occupied by the houses of the
Canons of the Cathedral.

Size and splendour are the outstanding characteristics, and the
dining-hall is the largest and most glorious in Oxford. Wolsey built it,
and Henry VIII dined here in self-satisfied state after the disgrace of
the Cardinal and the seizure of his college by the King. Though Henry
must have thought he had successfully obliterated the very name of
Wolsey, he failed. Wolsey's portrait hangs to-day alongside Henry's,
and the college emblem is still the Cardinal's hat. In Christ Church
Hall hangs an unrivalled series of portraits, eminent men of every
country. The great Tudors, Henry and his daughter Elizabeth, painted
by Holbein, are the chief pride, but all along the walls hang portraits
of eminent men of every century. Great painters are represented by
these works, Lely, Kneller, Reynolds, Gainsborough. Specially striking
perhaps is Romney's wonderful portrait of John Wesley, and another
most interesting face is that of the philosopher John Locke, pale and
thoughtful. But a more popular favourite is Lewis Carroll, whose
gentle intelligent face once caused an enthusiastic girl visitor to burst
out, " If he'd been alive to-day I should have fallen in love with
him."

Christ Church Hall is indeed glorious, and you reach it by a staircase which generally wins more admiration than other of Oxford's
sights. The roof with its exquisite fan-vaulting is supported by one
solitary pillar, springing slender and graceful from the base of the
stairs, and it is hard to believe this delicate column bears the whole

weight of the vaulted ceiling. Yet the architect of this marvel is almost forgotten and few know that " Smith " built it in 1640.

Besides the great hall, the only other part of Wolsey's vast projects to be completed by him, and to survive, is the block of kitchens and cellars which were to deal with the important matter of food and drink. Why they were given priority we do not know. History remembers Wolsey as the rich, ostentatious, gorgeous Cardinal, overbearing, worldly and much given to organizing magnificent entertainments to please his Sovereign. So perhaps it is fitting that alone of all his dreams for his college, there survives intact this gigantic range of kitchens. They are indeed famous, and in some ways justly. There the centuries-old tables are still used, the bake-houses still exist, the old spits and racks are still to be seen.

Come out of these homely quarters, for homely they really are in spite of their scale, and as you step out into the air and space of the quadrangle, your mind is caught up again by the realization of beauty. For in the centre is the lily-pool, and there, balancing with foreign grace, stands the statue of Mercury, poised above the lilies and the gold-fish. Oxford gives you another of her contrasts, another example of the determination, too, of youth to " make a mock of serious things ". For to the young men of Christ Church, Mercury is not just a charming piece of statuary, but may almost be called a " moral " force. When any individual has made himself, by his behaviour, intolerable to his fellow-undergraduates of the college, he is seized upon and thrown into the pool, and in this way has pointed out the error of his ways and the need to improve them.

Samuel Johnson, who was himself at Pembroke opposite, had a most touching connexion with Christ Church. He had come to Oxford in 1728, terribly poor. He wished to get notes of some lectures given by a celebrated man in Christ Church, and used to come across to a friend who as an undergraduate of the House could attend. But Johnson was so penniless that when his shoes wore out, and he saw that this humiliating circumstance was perceived by the Christ Church man, he came no more. He was so proud that, someone having set a pair of new shoes by his door, he threw them away with indignation. A happier touch is given when we find that on being asked by the

G 551

St. Edmund's Hall

authorities why he had stopped going to his tutor for his weekly class, he explained that he had spent his time " sliding " in Christ Church Meadows, for, as he told Boswell, "I did not benefit by my tutor's instructions, indeed I did not attend him much."

Oxford's Cathedral, as we have said, forms part of Christ Church. Wolsey indeed pulled down the end of the nave, so as to complete the walls of his quadrangle. So you must search for a small inconspicuous archway, close to the entrance of the dining-hall, go in through the small arched entrance, and you will find yourself transported to a world and a building far older than the college. Here was the shrine of the Saxon princess, St. Frideswide, patron saint of Oxford, to whom the Cathedral is dedicated. She fled from the pagan bridegroom her father had chosen for her to found a nunnery at Godstow. The shrine of the saint was destroyed in the Reformation, and for four centuries nothing marked even the traditional site. Then in the mid-nineteenth century, in a disused well, some fragments were found. These have been put together and the shrine recreated. The fragments have a special charm, for they are very early " naturalistic " carvings of sprays of foliage, and we can recognize with pleasure the oak, the ash, and the ivy, leaves and fruit. Nearby still stands the two-storeyed " watch-chamber " carved in wood, where the priest from above could keep guard lest anyone should venture to steal the treasures of gold and jewels that once adorned the shrine. Look up at the chancel roof, and you cannot fail to be moved by the delicate pendants, with the fans of the tracery radiating out, light as lace, and contrast that breath-taking lightness with the heavy Norman columns of the nave. How could Henry and Wolsey consider this lovely church as of less importance than the college which engulfed it?

Yet, though the great colleges may claim to be the pride of Oxford, with their gardens and the magnificence of their buildings, there are always some amongst both visitors and undergraduates who will find a greater pleasure in the gentler charm of the small colleges. Merton has its irregular courts, and the pride of its heart, " Mob Quad ". You have to penetrate to this through passages and round corners. In particular you will pass, as you go under a little arch to the right of the hall, a very small building, with a very steep roof. It is hardly to be

3   (G 551)

103571

LIBRARY
COLBY-SAWYER COLLEGE
NEW LONDON, NH 03257

noticed, so small and plain it is, yet this is the ancient Treasury, built thick and strong to resist both thieves and fire. Winding on through a narrow passage you find yourself in the tiny Mob Quad, as it is called, though no one knows why. This is the oldest quad in Oxford, for Walter de Merton had not such ambitious designs as had his contemporary Wykeham, and was content to build on a small scale, and so completed his buildings first. Along one side, on the second floor, runs the library, and the small lancet windows here were finished by 1378. Studying in such dimness must have been very difficult, so the college, after three hundred years, in Stuart times, added the charming latticed dormer windows. Mob Quad sometimes seems like something out of a slightly uncanny fairy-tale. It tends to be dark, it is almost always silent, it does not, as do most quads, call up the vision of cheerful young men, generation after generation, clattering about it and shouting from its windows. It is withdrawn, remote, and its smallness seems to bring with it an air of constraint. But it is quite unforgettable.

Corpus Christi, next door, recalls the old piety which originally inspired the learning—and the foundation—of these colleges. There in the centre of the first court—gravelled, not as is usual carpeted with the green of grass—a column rises into the sun, crowned with a pelican, the symbol of the church who will give her life-blood to sustain her members.

Turn the corner up Merton Street and you find on your right Oriel, which has many claims to our interest. One of its founders was Edward II, generally considered as one of the " bad Kings " of England. Indeed, some people can only say, as a recommendation, that he enjoyed agricultural pursuits, and was said to be one of the best " hedgers and ditchers " (when he chose to exercise his skill) in the England of the fourteenth century. Yet this man, vicious and weak as he was (who perhaps atoned for his misdeeds when he died an agonizing death, inflicted by his wife the cruel Isabella, and her lover, Mortimer, at Berkeley Castle), is still held in honourable remembrance by this college to which he gave benefactions. Every Sunday at the college evening service, the Provost reads the old " bidding prayer " giving thanks and honour, amongst others, to this unfortunate king, calling to remembrance not his misdeeds, but his good—and thus denying the cynical words Shakespeare puts into the mouth of Mark Anthony as he orates over Caesar's dead body: " The evil that men do lives after them, the good is oft interred with their bones." Oriel has seen to it that this shall not be so with Edward II. To this college came some of the great Elizabethans. Sir Christopher Hatton, who won the favour of Queen Elizabeth by his dancing, and Raleigh, that puzzling figure, part " company-promoter ", part patriot, who at least brought us the gift of tobacco from America.

A lighter piece of Oriel history concerns its tortoise. For many years Oriel has possessed one of these creatures, and has always taken such advantage of it as it can. So, a few years back, an undergraduate wished to call the attention of the world to the fact that the pair of tortoises which then ambled peacefully about the quad had achieved the distinction of hatching an egg. A notice was dispatched to *The Times*, and duly inserted by an unsuspicious, or unlearned, member of the staff: " At Oriel College, Oxford, to Mr. and Mrs. Testudo, a son "—testudo being the Latin for tortoise.

Memories of a more serious kind hang about Oriel. This was the home of the "Oxford Movement", that revival of religion which aimed at restoring, amongst other things, the ancient ritual to the Church of England. Newman was a Fellow here, and as Oriel has always held the presentation to the university church across the High Street, he was, at the early age of 27, made Rector of St. Mary's. There he preached, there he won his immense influence, while from his rooms in Oriel he helped to publish the famous Oxford tracts. Within the last year or two his own annotated copy of the Tract 95, which first really began his move towards the Roman Catholic Church, was found in the Provost's lodgings. His two portraits, one most beautiful as a young man, the other sad and worn as a Cardinal, hang in the senior common-room along with those of his friends, some of whom followed him in his charge, while others such as Keble and Pusey kept to the church which he and they had loved and wished to revivify.

So far, we have been occupying ourselves with largely Gothic build-ings. Now, as a change, let us visit Trinity. The magnificent view of the gardens through the great grille shows the splendid garden front, designed partly by Sir Christopher Wren, and it was he, too, who

helped to draw up the plans for the chapel, a building which is wholly
of the seventeenth century, both in design and feeling. Indeed, built
as it was in the days of Charles II, it is considered by some as resembling
that period in its apparent lack of religious feeling. The " garden
quad " as it is called, is not actually a quadrangle at all, for it has only
three sides. Wren perhaps thought this would look well, and he was
also influenced by the idea that an enclosed quad was not healthy, an
idea copied by a few other colleges such as Worcester. The glory of
Trinity Chapel is above all else its unequalled carvings. They are by
Grinling Gibbons, and Grinling Gibbons at his best. And such was the
spirit of the age of Charles II that the tomb of the founder is concealed
by a pair of cupboards, glazed so that the tomb can be seen, but
enclosed in order that the whole interior may harmonize. The
wonderful decoration over the entrance, and the two panels on each
side, come from the same master-hand, and the ceiling with its rich
plaster work completes the Jacobean design.

One cannot omit Trinity's neighbour, Balliol, the proud upholder
of a tradition of brilliant scholarship. But it must be said at once,
that however great the gifts of her sons, past and present, Balliol has
really no outer beauty. Actually she is one of the earliest colleges to
be founded. John de Balliol, one of the regents of Scotland in 1260,
committed some deed which caused the Church to order him to perform
penance. He was flogged at the door of Durham Cathedral, and then,
as a more permanent sign of his repentance, ordered to endow a " hos-
tel " at Oxford. He died before he could do this, but his widow, Devorguilla, carried out the promise. She gave lands to endow the college,
and only within the last few years did the college part with the last
portion remaining of the land given 800 years ago. But the old buildings were practically all swept away in the nineteenth century; only the
old dining-hall remains, used now as a small library, and a late fifteenth-
century room, also a library. The rest, including the quite agreeable
eighteenth-century frontage, were all pulled down. Balliol, founded
by a Scot, has always contained a large proportion of Scots amongst
its members, and possibly this accounts for the imitation Scottish-
baronial style of most of the present building. No one can admire it,
and yet no one can conceive how it could be improved.

The Old Clarendon Building and the Sheldonian Theatre

G 551

Go on along St. Giles, and you come to Balliol's northern neighbour St. John Baptist College, one which it has been said " everyone should visit ".   It is the last of the colleges to the north, and within living memory stood on the edge of fields and woodland.   But when, in the middle of the last century, the university altered its rule that Fellows of colleges must be unmarried and live in the colleges, a spectacular change took place.   Very many of the Fellows did wish to marry, but where were they to live?   St. John's owns most of the land of " north Oxford ", and seizing the opportunity at once built houses suitable for Fellows and their prospective families.   Built largely in " Victorian gothic ", with arched front doors, gables, turrets and an infinite variety of what modern taste has condemned, " north Oxford " has yet some charm of its own.   These houses look and are comfortable and well built.   They call up memories of the days of large families, solid furniture, solid comfort.   Spring, too, makes this part of Oxford beautiful with flowering trees.   Laburnum, lilac, red may, cherries pink and white blaze from every garden.

So St. John's College itself is now the last ancient building before the miles of red brick begin which stretch out towards the country, save only for the little church just beyond, which is dedicated to St. Giles, saint of all travellers, who used to give thanks there on reaching the city.   St. John's chief glory is its garden, but if you are tired of plain grey walls, or gothic cloisters, here is a lovely Renaissance arcade, unlike anything else in Oxford.   As Laud, who built this quad, was one of the great supporters of Charles I, he completed his work by placing above the arcade two magnificent statues in bronze of Charles I and Queen Henrietta Maria.

Three hundred years after St. John's was built, Victorian zeal and piety set up a college nearby, originally set aside for those who were to take Holy Orders in the Church of England, a rule now given up. Keble for long has been regarded as a horrifying specimen of Victorian architecture.   Time has to some slight extent modified the colouring of its red, blue and white brick-work, but almost all Oxford was astounded when a few years back a body of eminent French architects and archæologists visited the city and expressed their warm approval of Keble.   They are reported to have said that Europe contained many

better specimens of Gothic, Renaissance and eighteenth-century architecture than Oxford can produce; Keble, however, they said (rightly)
was unique, and they went so far, it is alleged, as to say that future
generations would visit Oxford chiefly to see " this gem ". Such an
opinion must shake one's ideas of " taste ", and yet it is true that the
proportions of the college, and especially those of the chapel, are
good. Sometimes in an autumn evening, when the mists from the river
rise up, the dusk and mist veil the colours of Keble's bricks. Then
the chapel is silhouetted against the sky, and it is possible perhaps
to understand the opinions of those eminent Frenchmen.

Now we have, perhaps unconsciously, been following the develop-
ment and change of English architectural styles, the Gothic, Tudor
and Jacobean. There exists, however, a number of buildings in Oxford
deliberately based on a foreign tradition, the " classical " style taken
from Greece and Rome. One of the most successful adaptations of this
sort is found in The Queen's College, its rightful name, though it is
popularly shortened to " Queen's ". Her classical front stands boldly
and conspicuously in the High Street. Inside again are classical colon-
nades, and those, seen at night, with the effect of strong light and shade
produced by the round-headed arcades, carry the imagination back to
a very different world. Queen's has, however, despite its classical air, a
special link with plain Old English Oxford. For here, at Christmas,
takes place the ceremony of the Boar's Head. On Christmas Eve the
college holds this feast. It is traditionally said to commemorate the
feat of a member of the college who, in the ancient days when England
was still inhabited by wild and fierce animals, was wandering over the
woods of Shotover Hill, deep in the study of a volume of Aristotle.
Suddenly to his horror a wild boar rushed out of the thicket, and the
young man, having no weapon to hand, thrust his precious book down
the throat of the great ravening creature, and thereby choked it to
death and saved his own life. Whether he subsequently was able to
salvage his book we are not told. Whatever its origin, the ceremony
of the Boar's Head is both charming and interesting. The guests as-
semble in the dining-hall, the Provost and Fellows file in, and take their
places at the High Table; from the open arches above the entrance to
the hall a fanfare of silver trumpets rings out, the doors are opened,

and in comes the procession. A boar's head is even to-day large and very heavy, and carried as it is on a great silver dish, with all its decorations, it takes two men to carry it on their shoulders. They advance, with the choir, singing the old carol of " The Boar's Head in hand we bear ". They advance slowly and put the great dish down before the Provost. The Boar's Head is decorated with gilded sprays of bay and holly, and the Provost, breaking some of these off, distributes them to all who go up to receive them. Then the guests disperse, the doors are closed, and Provost and Fellows are left to their feast.

Perhaps it is a good idea to group Oxford's " classical " buildings together. Stand by the Martyr's Memorial and you will see across the road the most strictly classical building in Oxford, the Ashmolean Museum, with great pillared portico, carved pediments, and statues copied from the ancients adorning the balustrades and roof. When Oxford was first floodlit experts were asked to select one building to be floodlit by the university as a whole, in addition to whatever the separate colleges undertook. They chose the Ashmolean, where the effect obtained by the brilliant sunshine of Greece and Rome can be reproduced, and the strong light throws strong shadows and gives indeed a most striking and beautiful effect.

Look next along the charming vista of Beaumont Street, with its elegant flat-fronted houses, its graceful balconies of wrought iron, its tall windows, and doorways with their attractive fanlights. At the end of this pleasing street the view is closed by the grey pile of Worcester College. The site of the college was originally occupied by Benedictine monks, in 1283, but after the dissolution of the monasteries by Henry VIII, though efforts were made to found a college here, none succeeded until in 1714 a wealthy baronet of Worcestershire left his fortune to set up a college for the men of that county. So the new college was built in early eighteenth-century classical style, arcades, pediments and all. Luckily perhaps the idea proved too expensive for the money available; the quadrangle was never completed and the little row of fourteenth-century rooms (" mansions " they were called) still survives, with over every doorway a shield showing how each one was an offshoot of an abbey—Westminster and St. Albans being the most famous. Glance in at the open doors of these little houses, and you will see incredibly small steep oak staircases, leading up to the rooms above. So narrow are they that the bottom step has been cut away on each side to enable the door of the tiny rooms on the ground floor to open outwards—the cut-away bottom step thus forming a regular trap for the feet of anyone rushing down too quickly.

Beyond this enchanting little row, hidden away in Oxford's favourite style, is a little door, apparently leading only to a covered way. But go through the tunnel-like arch, and you suddenly find yourself in one of the most beautiful of all Oxford gardens, for Worcester has the proud distinction of having within its grounds a lake. Here in the summer term you may enjoy one of Oxford's treats. For the O.U.D.S. (Oxford University Dramatic Society) each year acts one of Shakespeare's plays out of doors. A different college is chosen each year, but naturally the society tends to pick out those best adapted as a background. New College with its wall and leafy mound is good, Magdalen can lend the deer park to give enchantment and reality to " forest scenes " such as those in *As You Like It*. But Worcester of course excels in the plays where water is important, as in *The Tempest*. Each university generation has its own ideas, and its own style for producing Shakespeare—but it is hardly possible not to score a success with Worcester's lake. The " Galleon " of *The Tempest* can advance across the water, ship-wrecked sailors can clamber up, realistically wet. No one who has seen it ever fails to yield to the magic of the scene as darkness begins to fall. A thrush will be pouring out its night song from one of the tall trees, the lake will glimmer and shine, and always the swans will float majestically into view, often moving in and out of the beams of light as if fully aware of their beauty.

GARDENS

Thoughts of Worcester lake inevitably turn the mind to another side of Oxford's loveliness—her gardens. We have had enough perhaps of streets and buildings, and the beauty of stone. Oxford is rich also in the beauty of outdoor things—flowers, grass, trees and water.

Not all of the colleges have gardens, some have only their quads, but amongst those who do possess them, some have outstanding attractions. New College generally finds special favour. The background of the old city wall with its ramparts and semicircular towers is in itself lovely. It is set off by the herbaceous borders which run along its length—some of the most artistic borders to be found anywhere. Then, too, from the middle of the grass rises the "mound", dating from Tudor times, its sides clothed with shrubs, and its summit crowned with trees. Behind this lies a quiet walk, shaded by tall limes, and you can look up to the tower and church of the ancient St. Peter's-in-the-East. The garden combines so many things, and does it perfectly. Besides all this, it is entered through a tall wrought-iron gate and screen which is almost unsurpassed both for the beauty of its design and its superb workmanship. This was made in 1684, and all must exclaim at the scene before them when they come through the inner archway of the great front quad and see the wonderful gate, with beyond its bars the blaze of flowers, the green turf and then the ancient wall.

St. John's, too, has a celebrated garden, very varied and very large. The Canterbury Quad, with its delicate Renaissance arcading, gives you, through an archway, a glimpse of green, and coming out to the garden you see an immense lawn, stretching away, its surface smooth and velvety, with trees bordering both sides and closing the vista. Hidden behind a screen of flowering shrubs lies a smaller enclosed space. Here is the famous rock garden, to which members of the college have for years sent rare plants from all parts of the world.

It was laid out by one of the Fellows as his pride and joy, and its arrangement of rocks and plants is wonderful. Bright flower-beds set in grass face the rock garden, and then the path winds out to what is called " the wild garden ". When, in summer, you turn back across the great lawn, you see the whole garden-front of the college, with its gables and five great oriel windows, the walls smothered in wistaria, roses, and every kind of flowering climber. The skill with which this whole garden has been planned is so great—for it is the true " landscape gardening " —that some have said it is the work of one or other of the most celebrated landscape gardeners of times past, either Repton or " Capability " Brown.

Trinity, which has its front quad planted with apple trees, like an orchard, has also a " garden quad ", which you see through the famous iron gates in Parks Road. These gates are kept closed, so legend says, until a Stuart sovereign shall reign again in England. Through the grille you see a long expanse of turf, bordered with flower-beds and trees, and far away across that green expanse (the biggest lawn in Oxford) the lovely mellow walls of the college, creeper-covered and in autumn glowing with red and yellow tints. Trinity garden has, too, a famous walk, covered with the arched branches of " pleached " lime trees, and this leafy spot was called " Daphne " in the days when the courtiers and ladies walked here during the Civil War.

These are " gardens full of flowers ", but there are other gardens whose glory lies not in flowers, but in trees. Thus Wadham remains in the memory as a place of green trees, and above all it conjures up the vision of its great purple beech. This garden too has rareties, sent back by Admiral Wills in the last year of the eighteenth century, to his brother the Warden—tulip tree, with pale green flower, Judas tree, covered in pink-purple bloom, even the rare " Ginkgo " (the maidenhair tree) are all here. And Queen's has a tiny perfect garden, " The Nun's Garden ", whose greatest beauty can be seen when it is full of the pink and white of great apple trees, and the petals shower down on little low grey walls bordering the tiny lawn, or the narrow beds filled with tulips.

One other garden will give great pleasure. Opposite Magdalen Tower, by Magdalen bridge, lie the " Botanic Gardens " as they are

called to-day, their old name being the " Physic Gardens ", for they
were intended for the growth of herbs and medicinal plants.   You
enter them by a grand gateway, designed by Inigo Jones, with niches
holding the statues of Charles I and Charles II, both so intimately
connected in history with Oxford.   A stone tablet on the wall hard by
tells you that this was once the burial-place of the Jews.   The gardens
have an enchanting situation.   Along one side runs the river, in summer
laden with punts and canoes which have set out from the boat-house
by the bridge.   Across the river are meadows, while willow trees and
great pink and red may trees hang down over the waters.   The gardens
themselves are planted with trees of all kinds, and the broad gravel
walks lead beneath their shade to pools with tall iris and different-
coloured water-lilies and lotus.

If you begin to long for freshness and peace, and are perhaps tired
of streets and colleges, go down to Christ Church Meadows.   These
lie all along the river bank from Folly Bridge, and through them runs,
too, the little branch of the river called " The New Cut ", which leads
to the river Cherwell.   You can go into the meadows by the Broad
Walk, where an avenue of glorious huge trees runs from the college
walls down to the river.   You can wander along the banks of the Isis
and look across meadows, in summer-time golden with buttercups,
where cows and sheep still graze.   And beyond the meadows,
looking back, you will see what is perhaps the most beautiful view in
Oxford—the whole long stretch of grey walls, rising from the meadows,
with beyond the splendid mass of Christ Church, the great tower and
the spire of the cathedral, and then, one beside the other, the spires of
the City Church and of St. Mary's, the immense bulk of Merton
Tower, the gables and roofs of Corpus Christi, and at the end, the
grace of Magdalen rising from the trees.   You will not hear the
sound of traffic, only occasionally the sound of bells.   It is a place of
incredible peace and beauty, and gives to many their most outstanding
impression of an Oxford still untouched by modern times.

Another charming walk is to be found in the University Parks.
You can reach them from the New Bodleian by walking along the
pleasant broad tree-lined road past Wadham and Rhodes House.   The
little river Cherwell runs through the Parks, its banks all overhung with

willows. A high graceful single-arched bridge spans the river, and you can cross to the meadow walks, and range as far as Old Marston, with its ferry-boat, and the little old-fashioned inn down by the riverside. There are swans which nest in the reeds of the Cherwell, and you may see them in summer leading their brood of grey cygnets in and out past the boats that float along in the sunshine. Or, if you are early about, you may be lucky enough to see the flash of blue as kingfishers dart to and fro. The Cherwell winds its way right up to Water Eaton, and is lovely in every part, and is in turn much loved.

Oxford in summer means " the river " to many, and if you go up the Cherwell in punt or canoe, on a fine afternoon, you see a different Oxford. You can start from Magdalen Bridge, and the river, branching off from the Isis, will take you right along through the meadows. There you will have enchanting glimpses of towers and spires rising in the distance above the bordering trees. One part of the Parks is a narrow walk, with trees arching over, that runs between two branches of the Cherwell, and hence is called " Mesopotamia " (between two rivers), and at the end is an old water-mill and a deep pool. This Oxford walk is specially lovely in spring, when the may trees are in flower, and there are yellow water-lilies floating on the river, but it is lovely too in autumn, when the leaves are yellow on the trees and the faint mist covers the meadows, and at all times it is peaceful and cool.

JACK MERRIOTT

A Corner of Magdalen College and Grounds

G 551

LIBRARIES, GLASS, TREASURIES

There are more specialized joys for those who have a taste for them. You may like books and libraries, or you may have a love for stained glass, or you may like treasures of old gold and silver. All these tastes can be gratified.

Libraries

As to libraries, besides the unsurpassed Bodleian there are others, of different character, to satisfy you—Merton, Queen's, the Codrington. Of the Bodleian we have already spoken, but those who do not care to visit it as a library should go there to pay however brief a visit to the old Divinity School, and visit it not only for its architectural perfection, but for the history which is bound up with its rooms.

Enter through what has been called " a miracle of architecture ", the main hall, with one of the most wonderful of all vaulted roofs, rich with elaborate ribs, and with great carved pendants, unsurpassed in style and effect. Go on beyond this hall, and you come to a smaller room, panelled and plain, the Convocation House. This is indeed a place of memories. For here in 1554 came Archbishop Cranmer, with Bishops Latimer and Ridley, to " dispute " with a body of Catholic clergy before Cardinal Pole, newly returned to England to re-establish Catholicism. Cranmer, Ridley, and Latimer were to attempt to defend their Protestant views, and the " disputation " was held in this Convocation room. Not succeeding in their defence they were condemned. All three were at first imprisoned in the old prison called Bocardo, in the Cornmarket, near the Church of St. Mary Magdalen. When alterations were made in the shops on this site a few years ago, traces of the cells were found. At the end of the year, the two Bishops were burned at the stake. Cranmer was to live another six months, and to endure greater disgrace. He had in the days of Henry VIII been consecrated by the Pope, and only later had he become a Protestant. He was

45

therefore to be tried by the representative of the Pope, Cardinal Pole. He was duly tried and condemned in St. Mary's Church. His courage failed him when he recalled the dreadful torments he knew Ridley and Latimer had suffered, and he gave way and recanted his beliefs and acknowledged he had erred. Even this could not save him. Mary Tudor was resolved on the death of the man who had brought about the divorce of her mother Catherine of Aragon from Henry VIII. So Cranmer was again taken to the Church of St. Mary, there to repeat aloud before a great congregation his recantation. By now he knew death by burning would follow at once upon this, and at the very last he resolved to stand firm. He mounted the little platform erected against one of the pillars, but instead of acknowledging his errors against Rome, he reaffirmed his belief in the Protestant religion, and went to his death.

Convocation room has witnessed other famous scenes. In 1682, when Parliament was called in Oxford by Charles II, the Commons sat there, and the Lords in a room of the great tower, and here Charles played his famous trick upon the Commons. For, towards the end of his reign, Charles was struggling with his Parliament, and decided that he would leave London and its mob, and summon Parliament (as he had a right to do) at Oxford instead of at Westminster. He then played a glorious trick. The two Houses were meeting in the precincts of the Bodleian, the Commons sitting in the small hall where 100 years before Cranmer had struggled for his life before Cardinal Pole. Charles himself went down to the room where the House of Lords sat, wearing his ordinary clothes. He secretly meant to dissolve Parliament and set himself free from their interference and opposition. But the King can only dissolve Parliament while wearing his robes of state. Charles sent across the courtyard to summon the Commons, and they, knowing he was not in state attire, came bustling across to the room in the tower, firmly believing the King meant to give way to them. But Charles—whose amusement we can imagine as he watched them come—had outwitted them. He had sent his robes down separately in a sedan-chair, from Christ Church, and to their horror when all assembled, Charles entered in his robes of state, dissolved Parliament and sent them off. The Bodleian therefore has its memories, tragic and gay.

If you are one of those who love books, and to whom a library truly appeals, you will find in Merton the oldest library in Oxford, and one of the most picturesque. It is small and dark, and the old oak staircase and arch, the ancient bays for books, the dimness and the rows of great folios, do above all give the feeling of antiquity. Here is a library which has been used for six hundred years. Here are great books, still chained to the book-cases, as they were in old times when books were rare, lest anyone should steal such treasures. Here is a little volume with dried flowers, and those flowers were picked in the days of Queen Elizabeth. Here is the original " Writ for the collection of ship-money " which drove Hampden to protest and to take up his struggle against the " arbitrary taxation " of Charles I. And you may be told of the ghost of Duns Scotus, the famous medieval philosopher, who was a member of Merton, and who is said to come at night to study once more in the library—a suitable pursuit for a learned ghost.

All Souls, too, has a famous library, the Codrington, housed in a most impressive great room, with marble floor, a beautiful ceiling, and with tall galleries running round. This is specially famous for its collection of law books, since All Souls has special attractions for lawyers. Indeed here it is necessary to explain something of All Souls, which is a constant puzzle to those who do not know Oxford. Visitors will ask wonderingly, " Is it true that All Souls has no undergraduates?" The answer is Yes, that is so. For the members of this college are men who have ceased to be undergraduates, and who have already got their degrees. Each year an examination is held, in the subjects of law and history, and the most brilliant undergraduates in the university go in for this. Two are selected, and they are given Fellowships. This means they receive £300 a year for five years, to enable them to qualify for a profession or to carry on research. Other Fellows are elected from men who are eminent. So All Souls has only " Fellows ", no undergraduates, and when its members meet together they are held to represent many of the best intellects in the country.

Once in a century, indeed on the first day of a new century, All Souls holds its own special feast. The site of the college was said to have been decided by a mallard (wild duck) settling there. So at the beginning of each century the Fellows meet and hold a feast, and then go in procession over the roofs of the college, climbing up and down, by the light of lanterns, singing the " Mallard Song ".

Now go farther along the High Street and you will come to Queen's. It was founded in the fourteenth century by Robert Eglesfield, chaplain to Queen Philippa, that Queen who is said to have begged the lives of the burghers of Calais from her husband King Edward III. Eglesfield, in honour of his mistress, called his college " The Queen's ", and whenever a queen of England comes to Oxford, she visits the college and is its guest of honour, even if the King himself comes with her. In the library there is a contemporary wooden statue of Queen Philippa, and in the dining-hall of the college there hang portraits of the Queens who have visited here. This library is certainly one of the great glories of Oxford. The tall wooden bays and shelves have the most exquisite carvings and end-pieces by Grinling Gibbons; the ceiling is of wonderful plaster-work; the round-headed windows, with wreaths and swags of moulded plaster-work above them, throw floods of light on one of the most beautiful rooms in the world.

Stained Glass

Medieval glass is found in all its beauty at Merton Chapel, the windows of the chancel being some of the earliest in Oxford. Here, too, before the 1939–45 war, the east end was a seventeenth-century window, painted in glorious shades of gold and brown. This was considered by experts to clash with the medieval windows, and when the glass, which had been taken to safety, was restored at the end of the war, this window was removed. But to some it seemed that the large size of the chancel needed the glow and warmth of this later work, and in general now, though to those who have studied the subject the old windows are of great beauty, perhaps the chapel does seem a little lacking in colour. Across at Magdalen you used to find strange windows in the ante-chapel, painted in shades of grey, black and white in the days of the Stuarts, but these windows, unique and interesting, have not been replaced since the 1939–45 war.

New College Chapel has three claims to interest in regard to its glass. The north and south sides of the great ante-chapel have the original fourteenth-century glass, a magnificent sight. The great west

window is filled with the famous glass designed by Sir Joshua Reynolds
(and is therefore called the Reynolds window). It is painted in shades of
gold, yellow and brown. In the village church out at Kidlington you
will see the same designs of the lower range of figures carried out in
colour, and you may understand why Reynolds kept to brown and
gold for the chapel. The top part of the Reynolds window shows
the Nativity, the lower, and more celebrated part, the seven virtues, pic-
tured as rather elegant seventeenth-century women representing Faith,
Hope, Charity and so on. These, though beautiful in themselves,
have not much religious feeling, and do not seem especially appropriate
when compared with the medieval windows which surround them.

During the 1939–45 war the whole window was taken down for
safety, and clear glass substituted. The light which then flooded the
chapel seemed far too brilliant and brought home how marvellously
the colour of painted glass enriches and softens. The chapel proper—
that is to say the part beyond the organ screen—has ugly glass of a
late period. But here a guide may, if he thinks it suitable, call your
attention to the end window on your left as you enter the chapel. This
represents Adam and Eve, originally clothed in nothing but a few fig
leaves. Some Victorian worthy evidently considered this to be an
unsuitable sight for the eyes of the undergraduates, who sit in this
part of the chapel, and had the figures painted over with draperies.
But if you look, you can still see the fig leaves.

Another chapel has glass which, while having interest and artistic
merit, is also amusing. University College chapel has its windows
filled with very remarkable glass. It was made by two brothers, Dutch-
men called Bernard and Abraham Van Ling. They had fled from the
persecution of the Dutch by the Spaniards, and came to Oxford in
1610. The colours are very deep and intense, orange, purple, green, all
in deep glowing tones. The subjects in the main chapel are taken from
the old Testament, and it is a test of biblical knowledge to identify them
all. The artist's sense (or perhaps his lack) of humour can be seen
where Sarah is " laughing behind the door ", or in the panes where
Jonah is being thrown to the whale from a Tudor galleon flying the
college flag. One may also observe, in the ante-chapel, a window
where Martha, tired of " much serving ", is angrily brandishing what

4   (G551)

is quite clearly a colander, such as is used in the modern kitchen to-day.

The Van Lings painted a very fine east window at Wadham, and in the Cathedral, to the left of the door as you go in, is another by them in the same style as the University Chapel, of Jonah sitting under the gourd, again full of life and incident. The Cathedral has some specially beautiful early glass. In the north chapel there are most beautiful windows, with a lovely tint of green, and indeed all this north side has delicate early glass, full of beauty. If you cross to the south chapel (the Memorial Chapel to the Oxford and Bucks Light Infantry) and look at the tracery at the top of the chapel's east window, you will gradually make out a scene famous in history. The little panels show the murder of St. Thomas-à-Becket, with the knights who did that deed. When Henry VIII destroyed and pillaged the shrine of St. Thomas at Canterbury, he also ordered that all representations of St. Thomas, and specially his murder, should be destroyed over the length and breadth of England. These tiny panes with their vivid representation escaped destruction, either because being so small they were not noticed, or perhaps because they were high enough up to be difficult to reach.

And, finally, if you like to compare medieval with modern, you can see a whole set of windows by Burne Jones in the chapel of Manchester College, close by Holywell, and decide whether they compare well with the work done so many centuries ago.

Treasuries

If you have inclination, and time, to look at wonderful old silver and gold, the colleges have great treasure to show you. In New College Chapel you can see William of Wykeham's crozier (or Bishop's staff), inlaid with jewels and richly enamelled. In the Treasury (open once a week to visitors), which has one of the richest and most famous collections of plate in Oxford, besides the unique college plate, you can see his mitre. This was only discovered recently, and by chance, for no record of its existence was known. When one of the last Wardens died, his successor cleared out the " box-room ", and in a modern Victorian hat-box, opened casually, was Wykeham's fourteenth-century mitre, set with rubies and emeralds and entirely covered with pearls. When we realize that the cost of merely resewing those pearls was many hundreds of pounds, we can understand the priceless character of this relic.

Christ Church and Magdalen, too, have wonderful plate, but too many of the colleges gave theirs to be melted down for King Charles I. Queen's has a celebrated drinking horn, given by the founder in the fourteenth century, which is produced on great feast days and the Fellows in turn drink from it and pledge each other. All Souls, too, has ancient mazer bowls and the jewelled and enamelled pins shaped almost like flowers, used in medieval times to adorn a bishop's mitre. These are probably unique and belonged to Archbishop Chichele. Such great treasures as these are naturally kept securely locked away, and are only on view on special days, or special occasions, but every college uses some of its beautiful silver pieces daily, setting them out at evening to adorn the High Table.

GREAT MEN AND WOMEN OF THE PAST

A countless stream of men and women has flowed through Oxford, and the sense of a continuous life is very strong. It is the multitude of ordinary men who have made university life, but in addition Oxford has connexions with the great of all ages. She has many links with the past, and stories and legends which go far back across the centuries.

Alfred the Great used to be claimed as the founder of University College, partly because of his known love of learning, partly from a mistaken interpretation of a document produced in a legal dispute. But imaginary as that idea proved to be, Oxford actually has a link with the Saxon King. For in the Ashmolean Museum is preserved " Alfred's Jewel ". This is a pale green transparent stone, carved with a representation of the Almighty, and set in a very wide gold orna-mented band ending in a wolf's head, with the inscription in Anglo-Saxon " Alfred had me made ". The jewel is vouched for by all experts as genuine. It was not worn, as so many think, as a pendant; it was a tassel, or weight for the book-marker of some holy book. " Alfred had me made " shows this was really made for the king. It was found in the seventeenth century on farm-land near the Isle of Athelney, which in Alfred's day was a huge marsh. Alfred hid there after his early defeat from the Danes, and we can imagine perhaps the horror and grief which would seize him when he found his jewel gone. For there is no record of it anywhere, from the days of Alfred in 967 right down to the finding of the jewel, so we can but imagine it was lost in those wanderings, not to be found till 700 years had passed. Yet it is as bright and clear to-day as it was then. So famous is this jewel that, when the treasures of the museum were sent away for safety during the second world war, the museum had an exact replica made, so that the thousands of American and European visitors who would come, wishing to see the original, should at least see exactly what it looked like.

After Alfred's days, the Danes did conquer England, and the great Danish king, Canute, came to Oxford in 1018, and there he had his son crowned (though the son never succeeded to his father's kingdom), showing that Canute considered Oxford as one of the greatest cities of the day. After Canute the Dane came the Normans.

In 1100 we have the romantic story of Queen Matilda, the grand-daughter of William the Conqueror and heiress to the throne. Having taken refuge in the great castle tower, she soon saw that her forces were not strong enough to hold the castle against her enemy Stephen. England had never had a Queen, and Stephen declared himself King. But Matilda had a baby son, and even if a woman could not reign, she claimed that her son, great-grandson of William the Conqueror, could. So, to save the child, she fled from the castle, and escaping across the snow, found safety. That child grew up to become one of the greatest of our early kings, Henry II, and he gives Oxford her claim to be the scene of a famous story. For in later life Henry did not love his wife —the proud, violent Eleanor of Aquitaine. Legend says that he loved " Fair Rosamund ", and hid her away in " Rosamund's Bower " near Binsey, a tiny hamlet across Oxford's great Port Meadow. There Eleanor traced her, and on a day when the king had departed, the queen stole in and forced Fair Rosamund to choose death " either by the dagger, or the poison bowl ". Binsey Church has an old well in its churchyard, known as the " Wishing Well ", and if you drop in a coin and touch the water, your wish should be fulfilled. But the old country people still give it another name and call it to this day " Fair Rosamund's Well ".

It is indeed a lovely walk to Binsey, across Port Meadow, that vast stretch of open ground to the north of the city which is still a pasture " held in common by the freemen of Oxford " and as such cannot be built over. Cross the river, and pass Binsey village green. From it a little lane wanders along for a short distance and brings you to the tiny church, standing quite alone, with Wytham woods beyond. The well is almost hidden in a corner of the churchyard, with bushes over-hanging it, on whose branches you will sometimes find rags fixed, an example really of the ancient worship of the trees, for these rags are tied there by country folk who believe in earlier rites than throwing coins in the well.

Henry II, if the story of Rosamund and Binsey be true, would have found it easy to visit Rosamund's Bower, since in those days the king owned a splendid palace, Beaumont Palace, and in the palace was born Henry's famous son, Richard of the Lion Heart. That palace has long since been destroyed, and no stone of it remains, but its name still is given to the street which runs where once Henry played with his boy.

Now leaving legend and romance we must return to Oxford and to true history. One of the most celebrated visitors to the university was that great sovereign Queen Elizabeth. She thoroughly enjoyed herself, for, indeed, being very highly educated, she could, and did, listen with pleasure and reply to the speeches in Latin and Greek with which she was greeted. She listened to disputations on philosophy, enjoyed the masques and dances and banquets arranged for her. She showed her tolerance by leaving untouched the two colleges founded under Mary by two Catholic baronets (Trinity and St. John's). She evidently enjoyed herself so much that she came again and ended her last visit with the words " Farewell, farewell dear Oxford, God bless thee and increase thy sons in number, holiness and virtue". Her visits were occasions of pleasure and amusement which filled streets and colleges with splendour and gaiety, a merry-making which seems to show in golden sunshine the riches and stability of Elizabethan England.

Poor James I, who followed Elizabeth on the throne, did not enjoy his visits as she did. He tried to sit out interminable entertainments, or rather performances that were intended to entertain him. But his interest and his strength failed him, and he fell asleep, waking to say crossly, " What sort of creature do they take me to be?"

After James, the scene began to darken, and the next royal visitor was to come when Civil War was casting its evil shadows over the land. For Oxford's most widely known connexion with historical events is the part she played in the Civil War between Charles I and the Parliament. Charles, after leaving London, made Oxford his headquarters, and here he and his court lived for four years (1642–46). Charles himself made Christ Church his headquarters. The queen, Henrietta Maria, had her lodgings at Merton. Prince Rupert came with his uncle. The King's Parliament met in the great hall of Christ Church, and New College stored the King's ammunition in her cloisters, while Charles himself would climb Magdalen Tower to spy out the enemy, camped on Shotover. Oxford was Royalist to the core, and for those four years the streets and quadrangles were filled with gloriously attired men and women, in their lovely silks and satins, their plumed and feathered hats. No more enchanting throng can ever have overflowed the old city. But though Parliament and the Roundheads could not, at that date, beat the king, one man in Oxford could. On December 30th, 1645, the king wished to borrow a book from Bodley's Library. Now the rule is (as laid down clearly by Bodley himself) that you may go and read any book you choose *in* his library, but no one may take a book away to read. The librarian therefore informed King Charles that no book could be taken out, even by the King himself, and Charles had to give way.

Many memories of this prolonged visit of king and court exist to this day. St. John's College has an elaborate statue of the King (by the great sculptor Le Sueur) in a niche in the centre of the Canterbury Quad, and opposite it a simpler and more lovely one of Queen Henrietta Maria. Merton still calls one of its passages " The Queen's Passage ", for it was the way by which she used to pass to visit her husband's quarters in nearby Christ Church.

It is easy to think of Oxford during the time when it was the King of England's court, with Queen Henrietta Maria and her ladies dressed in brilliant satin and silk, with becoming deep lace collars, their hair in soft curls and ringlets on their foreheads, or at night twisted with pearls; the men in equally colourful clothes, silk, satin and velvet—even when ready to go out to fight—silk sashes, and that most attractive of all head-dresses, the broad-brimmed hat with its great sweeping feather plumes. Charles himself was not handsome, but his nephew Rupert, with his strong dark face, was a striking, vivid personality. In those days, too, the Royalists were full of hope and gaiety. So Oxford colleges were inhabited by a brilliant crowd and never before or since can the city have witnessed such wonderful scenes.

Yet though one is apt to recreate an Oxford glowing with colour, with music of dances, or military trumpets sounding as Rupert led his men out to fight, it has to be remembered, too, that as those four years passed, the court must have lost much of its gaiety. Rejoicings and amusements must have died away as gradually it became clear that the King's cause was losing ground. In the royal circle quarrels broke out, and Rupert, bitterly estranged from the King, his uncle, must have spent unhappy hours in his rooms. At length all ended. Charles saw that he could no longer resist, he could only hope to escape, as the army of Parliament, under Fairfax, drew near. He had come into Oxford from the north, to be greeted by cheering crowds and welcomed by the university and city heads. He crept away, secretly, over Magdalen Bridge, disguised as a servant, his kingly splendour gone, riding over the bridge in his coarse grey clothes. Only three weeks later Rupert had to surrender the city to the Parliamentarians. Fairfax, recognizing Rupert's gallantry, let him depart with the honours of war, and with his few troops he too went out over Magdalen Bridge, in his case with trumpets blowing and flags flying.

When Charles had died on the scaffold and Oliver Cromwell became ruler of England, he came to the city which had been for so long the headquarters of the King, and we can picture to ourselves the feelings aroused by the visit of this very different ruler. Oliver took an interest in education and knew also that the universities played a great part in the life of those days. He had himself studied at Cambridge, but Cambridge had supported the Parliamentary cause, as had most of East Anglia, Cromwell's own country. Now he wished to swing Royalist Oxford into line. So, having first sent down cart-loads of pamphlets to " convert " the Oxford men and enable them to see the error of their ways, he next managed to have his chaplain, Owen, made Vice-Chancellor, and finally he himself was made Chancellor and came to Oxford in state to receive an honorary degree.

It should be explained that the Chancellor is the official head of the university, but he is not resident in Oxford. He is usually a man of eminence in the outer world, and comes to Oxford only for great occasions, when he wears magnificent robes of black and gold. The administration of the University is carried out by the Vice-Chancellor,

Oxford from Boar's Hill

G 551

who is chosen in rotation from the heads of the colleges. Eminent men who are not members of the University are given "honorary degrees" at a special ceremony held in the Sheldonian. It is one of the occasions when the doctors, professors and dignitaries come in procession, headed by the Vice-Chancellor with his attendant " beadles " carrying maces, and the sight of the coloured robes, some scarlet, some crimson, some blue and crimson, some primrose yellow, is gorgeous. The doctors take their seats in a semicircle, with the Vice-Chancellor in his great chair in the middle. The floor of the hall is filled with members of the University in their black gowns, and spectators go up to the two galleries above. When the sun slants down through the tall windows, and strikes on the circle of multi-coloured robes beneath, it is indeed a brilliant scene. Each candidate for an honorary degree is led up the aisle by the Public Orator, and stands before the Vice-Chancellor to be presented. The Public Orator makes a short speech in Latin, generally containing witty allusions to the qualifications or feats performed by the (sometimes embarrassed) candidate.

After receiving his honorary degree himself, the Protector, with General Fairfax, went on to Magdalen. There they dined and played a game of bowls as a finish to their day. At Magdalen he observed the fine organ, standing in the chapel, and as, under the Puritans, no music in churches or chapels was allowed, he had the organ transferred to Hampton Court Palace, where he then lived as head of the State. Some have looked on this as mere robbery, but Cromwell really loved music, and the organ was safe at Hampton Court, where it was used for the concerts Oliver enjoyed and where it is to this day.

After Oliver's death came the Restoration, and to Oxford in his turn came Charles II. His court was very different from that of his father. Indeed Charles, as usual, did not scruple even on these state visits to bring with him, as well as his unfortunate Queen, his reigning mistresses. On his first visit (1663), besides the Queen he brought the beautiful Barbara, Lady Castlemaine. When London was ravaged by the Great Plague he came again to Oxford. He himself lodged at Christ Church, and he brought the Queen and Lady Castlemaine, besides the girl whom he tried in vain to win, Frances Stuart, and his eldest illegitimate son, Monmouth. Lady Castlemaine, whilst lodging at Merton, gave birth to a son, later founder of one of our great ducal families. We can imagine that, surrounded by his companions, Charles II held revelry very different from the dignified enjoyment of Queen Elizabeth, and that the court he kept was totally unlike that of his father, Charles I.

Very different was the scene of the next royal visit. The House of Hanover brought with it to England all the rigid etiquette of a small German court, and imposed rules of behaviour very different from those England had hitherto known. George III came to Oxford in 1786, with his wife, the ugly little Queen Charlotte, and two of his daughters. Fanny Burney, then a lady-in-waiting, has given a vivid account in her " Diary ". George came to receive a loyal address, congratulating him on his escape from assassination. The royal procession went to the Sheldonian, where the King occupied the high seat at the top of its short steep flight of wooden steps, and the university dignitaries were to come up in turn and kiss his hand. This led to a truly ridiculous scene. Strict observers of etiquette, like old Lord Harcourt, tried to walk backwards down the steps, and Fanny shall give us her own account: " The sight at times was very ridiculous. Some of the worthies, unaccustomed to such ceremonies, the moment they had kissed hands turned their backs on the King and walked away; others, attempting to do better, did still worse, tottering, stumbling and falling foul of those behind. Some, ashamed to kneel, stood and took the King's hand straight up to their mouths, others plumped down on both knees and could hardly get up again, and many in their confusion fairly pulled his Majesty's hand to raise them." Indeed, though Fanny at first enjoyed the ceremonies and specially praised the coloured robes of the doctors, she goes on to give a heartrending description of the sufferings of the courtiers, men and women alike, from the hunger they endured. For court etiquette forbade anyone to eat in the presence of royalty, and as the long day went on, the ladies and gentlemen in waiting were obliged to stand, absolutely starving, while the King and Queen feasted at one meal after another. In Christ Church " a whisper was buzzed through of the deplorable state and presently it reached the ears of the worthy doctors ", who, coming to their assistance, smuggled in tea, coffee and chocolate, which was put on a table behind the King's circle, and " the good doctors soon by sly degrees and with watchful caution, covered it with tea, coffee, chocolate, cakes, bread and butter ". None of Fanny's companions had eaten since early morning, and "there was too much eagerness to seize the present moment ". One poor lady, Lady Charlotte Bertie, was actually standing all day with a sprained ankle and could scarcely crawl out of the hall. The evening closed with one of the men whispering to the exhausted ladies that they could " slip out into a little parlour belonging to the master of the college ", which they did, and one of the gentlemen produced from a paper concealed in his pocket, some apricots and bread. But alas! to their horror, while they were eating away as hard as they could, the queen came in! " Quick into our pockets we crammed our bread, close into our hands we squeezed our fruit "—and off they were dragged to Newnham Courtney, a long drive in those days, still famished and weary.

So the list of royal visitors goes on, and we may close with the visit of Queen Victoria, who came also to dine in Christ Church in the days when Lewis Carroll was one of the Fellows ranged there to receive her in Tom Quad.

How countless are the names of great and famous men who have stayed in Oxford! But none is more famous than Shakespeare. He travelled through on his journeys to and from London and Stratford-on-Avon. One of his closest friends kept the old Crown Inn, in the Cornmarket, near Carfax. Shakespeare stood godfather when little William Davenant was christened in old St. Martin's, and the font by which Shakespeare stood is now in the City Church close by. The Crown has disappeared, though its neighbour, the Golden Cross, still stands, and we can turn into its little courtyard and see the old walls with their Tudor timbering, and eat our meals in the little Tudor dining-room. A few years ago a very interesting discovery took place, when alterations were being made to the shop next door. A panelled room existed and it was found that behind this panelling was a " Painted Wall ", certainly there in Shakespeare's day. The wall is covered with a lovely design, beautifully clear and fresh, which strangely enough is rather oriental in character. You can stand in that room and reflect that Shakespeare once must have known it well.

Great men who have been members of the University are far too numerous to name, but we can pick out a few. As Oxford was originally founded on religious lines, let us begin with men of religion. Wyclif, the precursor of the Reformation, was Master of Balliol. Wolsey, almost the most famous of Oxford churchmen, came up from Suffolk as a scholar of Magdalen, and we have already described what he achieved for Oxford. Archbishop Laud was President of St. John's, and became Chancellor of the University. We can better understand why Laud was so hated by many people when we read of the rules he laid down as to the conduct of members of the university. They were " to abstain from that absurd practice of walking publicly in boots "— a hit, one imagines, at the long soft leather boots, in russet brown, coming nearly to the thighs, with turned down flapping tops, so dearly loved by the young Cavaliers. They were to be fined if they " wore curls, or immoderately long hair ", and here the archbishop was more severe than the Puritans, for Cromwell and his generals all wore their hair down to their shoulders. The young men at college were not to play dice, or cards, they were not to hunt with hounds, ferrets or nets; they might not go hawking, they were forbidden to play football or " cudgels "; they were not to " drive themselves in any vehicles "; and any stage-players or dancers, or fencers, coming to the university for gain, should be imprisoned. One hardly knows what amusements, if any, he would have allowed, yet Laud was no Puritan. He was a high-churchman and the bitter enemy of Puritanism. No one can think he wished for a " Merry England ". The modern university, as we know, takes a different view. What would Laud have thought of modern sports in Oxford, or of the University Dramatic Society, which now allows girl undergraduates to act together with the men? True it is, all theatrical efforts in which undergraduates take part in Oxford to-day still are " by permission " of the Vice-Chancellor, and the Proctors (two university officials chosen to supervise the behaviour of undergraduates outside their colleges) can intervene if any undergraduate behaves badly in public. While as to " driving in vehicles ", the modern undergraduate after his first year may have permission to have his own motor-car.

Long after Laud had gone to the scaffold, a very different man set out to achieve reform, in a very different way. John Wesley and his brother Charles were both at Christ Church, and it was at Oxford, with their friend, George Whitfield, that they began, with a little band of friends, to practise that " method in religion " which gave rise in the end to the first Wesleyan Movement.   Or you may think of Bishop Ken, who wrote the well-loved evening hymn, " All Praise To Thee My God This Night ", and the men of the nineteenth-century " Oxford Movement ", Keble, Pusey and Newman, or Bishop Hampden, hero of a now almost forgotten controversy, for Hampden was one of the nineteenth-century " Modernists ".   Gilbert White, too, that most lovable of naturalists, was an Oxford man.

Of special interest to the innumerable visitors from the United States is the fact that the great-great-grandfather of George Washington was an Oxford man.   He was at Brasenose College in 1619, and left owing the college the sum of 17s. 10d.—but why and for what, we do not know.   That debt remained in the college books for 300 years, until in 1914 it was paid by some American visitors.

Of writers, you may think of Shelley, wandering up Shotover Hill, or talking and arguing in his rooms; of Robert Browning, who was at Balliol; of Matthew Arnold, whose " Scholar Gipsy " reveals in every line an intense love of Oxford and the countryside around her. Gibbon was at Magdalen, and Locke the philosopher at Christ Church. Harvey, discoverer of the circulation of the blood, was an Oxford scholar. Their name is indeed legion.   Nor perhaps, in lighter vein, should we forget the Warden of New College at the end of the nineteenth century, Dr. Spooner, whose habit of twisting round words (" a half warmed fish " when he meant " a half formed wish ") has become a universal source of amusement in the form of the " spoonerism ".   One American lady, just before 1939, even came specially to Oxford to see where he had lived!   The great Elizabethan Sir Walter Raleigh was at Oriel, William Penn at Christ Church, Sir Christopher Wren, England's greatest architect, was at Wadham, Dr. Johnson at Pembroke.   Peel, Gladstone and many another statesman were Oxford men.

MODERN CHANGES

Oxford has changed a good deal in modern times, in certain distinct ways. She is no longer simply a university city, she is a manufacturing one. Lord Nuffield started life working in a small bicycle shop in Oxford, and when later he began to build up his great motor manufactory, he placed his works there, in the southern part called Cowley. (Hence the names given to his popular cars, Morris Oxford; Morris Cowley.) The creation of these great works has naturally altered the character of the city in some ways. The thousands employed have to be housed, and nowadays we are told that the bulk of Oxford's citizens live beyond Magdalen Bridge. Many deplore this industrialization of Oxford, but to set against that we may remember the great benefactions Lord Nuffield has given, especially to the study of medicine in Oxford.

Again, Oxford has tried to develop the " scientific " side of study, and to-day new ranges of buildings, laboratories and pathological research departments rise in great blocks along the Parks. These buildings do emphasize the " modern " element growing up alongside the old, and Oxford can deny she is " the home of lost causes " when she has forged ahead in these new paths.

She has shown herself progressive, too, with regard to the position of women in the university. In the later years of the nineteenth century a few pioneer women started the women's colleges, as they have now risen to be. At first only a handful, in private houses bought by enthusiasts, the girls who came were only allowed, by courtesy, to attend lectures. As numbers grew, they were eventually allowed to take the same final examination as the men, but it was not till the 1914-18 war that Oxford admitted women as full members, sharing all rights and privileges and being granted degrees. So the four women's colleges are modern buildings, and perhaps owing to the fact that they had small funds, and money came in slowly, their buildings are very piecemeal, wings and halls and chapels being added at different times, and in different styles. One college, St. Hilda's, has the good fortune to have secured one of the best sites in Oxford, lying just over Magdalen Bridge, with a garden sloping to the river, over which in spring hang great boughs of red hawthorn. Lady Margaret Hall provides much argument over its chapel built of red brick, and called by some " a piece of Byzantium dumped down by the Cherwell ".

Of course one of the main characteristics of Oxford's population is the tide of young people, men and girls, who in term time fill the streets. When they are going to lectures, or classes, or some other university activities, they must wear " academic " dress, which strictly speaking should mean they must wear " cap and gown ". In practice, for many years now, the young men have decided they will not wear " cap ". For the cap is really a stiff mortar-board, heavy and hot, and above all difficult to wear when bicycling against a wind. So, though on formal occasions it must be worn, it is now so rare that if sudden need arises, an undergraduate will have to search about to find someone who actually owns a " cap " and will lend it. These formal occasions are such affairs as " degree giving " or that worse ordeal, the viva-voce examination which is the last stage in the final examinations. For these the university declares " sub-fusc " (i.e. dark clothes) must be worn. Formerly it had to be black, but the war has relaxed this stern rule, and dark blue or dark grey is accepted now. " Gowns " vary. The quaint short black garment, with two flying streamers in front, is worn by the ordinary undergraduate, or " commoner ", and it is apt to be shabby and torn—perhaps to show the wearer is no newcomer just " up ". Scholars wear long full gowns, down to below the knee. It is amusing to see scholars—of both sexes—bicycling fast (much haste is necessary if you have to dash from one lecture to another), with their black gowns flying out and billowing in the wind. Both kinds of gowns are survivals from the dress worn by medieval scholars.

When women were given degrees, the question of " academic " dress gave rise to much heart-burning. For a stiff mortar-board, constructed to cling close to a man's cropped head, clearly would never fit a girl with clusters of curls piled up, or long thick coils of hair. Eventually it was decided that girl undergraduates should have a soft square black " cap ", really like the old Tudor cap, and this, if worn with dash, can be a most becoming affair. But any form of hat is usually discarded nowadays, and Oxford men and girls go happily about with bare heads. In the same way the " sub-fusc " of the girls has had to be adapted, but every woman member of the university, on formal academic occasions, must wear black or dark blue, and black stockings—and this need again often has to be met by frantic borrowing.

To-day girls and young men share in university life, in amusements as well as studies. Oxford has become in this respect like the outside world, and in a place originally meant only for men, the new companionship of men and girls is accepted. It is strange to live in Oxford and see how, when the vacations come and 5000 young people leave, and then when terms begin and back comes this flood of youth, the whole city seems to change. Possibly it is best to see Oxford in term time, for then you will be able to see young men (and girls too) in scanty shorts and bright scarves, dashing out of the colleges and rushing off on bicycles. Or you may feel you are in a different world if you catch a glimpse of dignitaries in their coloured robes making their way along, peacefully and sedately, to a ceremony or an official meeting. The grey buildings, the great trees in which Oxford abounds, seem a fitting background for both. Perhaps you may feel, as you see the old costumes still surviving and still worn, that they, as well as the stream of youth always coming and going, are symbols of the eternal vitality of Oxford.

Think, too, as you take your farewell of Oxford, that she has opened wide her doors now to everyone who wishes to learn. No longer can she be accused of being " the preserve of the rich ". The poorest of all can come. Scholarships from county educational authorities can cover the entire cost of university education, and indeed the greater proportion of men and girls alike to-day have grants. The " poor scholars " for whom she was originally founded have returned.

So you may take your leave of this beautiful city. Every kind of beauty is there—beauty of buildings made by man, beauty of nature in river, trees and flowers; and perhaps you have felt, as you trod where so many have trod before you, that both great men and obscure who have lived here, have known the beauties of the mind, have understood the things of the spirit, and have taken with them, out into the world, an imperishable heritage.

DA
690
.098
M87

103571
Muir, Dorothy.
   Oxford.

DATE DUE

SUSAN COLGATE CLEVELAND
LIBRARY/LEARNING CENTER
COLBY-SAWYER COLLEGE
New London, New Hampshire 03257

GAYLORD   PRINTED IN U.S.A.

← Pocket inside

OXFORD

Scale _ Six Inches to One Mile

Feet 0   500   1000 Feet

REPRODUCED FROM THE ORDNANCE SURVEY MAP, WITH THE SANCTION OF THE CONTROLLER OF H.M. STATIONERY OFFICE